T0376625

Chinese-Foreign Cooperation in Running Schools

During the past decade, transnational education has grown rapidly and become a key initiative of internationalization of higher education. In China, one of the main forms of transnational education is Chinese-Foreign Cooperation in Running Schools (CFCRS). In May 2017, there were 2545 CFCRS institutions and programs approved by the Chinese government. There are about 560,000 CFCRS students nationwide, among which 460,000 are in higher education, while graduate numbers have exceeded 1.6 million.

CFCRS has attracted more and more attention, and related studies have been increasing over the years. This book contains a comprehensive introduction and in-depth study on CFCRS, and includes comparative studies on the development of international branch campuses of several countries.

This book was originally published as a special issue of *Chinese Education & Society*.

Lin Jinhui is a Professor at Xiamen University, China. He is also Director of the Center of Research on Chinese-Foreign Cooperation in Running Schools (CRCFCRS). His research interests cover theory and practice of CFCRS, policy and management of CFCRS, and curriculum and teaching in CFCRS.

Chinese-Foreign Cooperation in Running Schools

Edited by
Lin Jinhui

LONDON AND NEW YORK

First published 2018
by Routledge
2 Park Square, Milton Park, Abingdon, Oxon, OX14 4RN, UK

and by Routledge
711 Third Avenue, New York, NY 10017, USA

Routledge is an imprint of the Taylor & Francis Group, an informa business

© 2018 Taylor & Francis

All rights reserved. No part of this book may be reprinted or reproduced
or utilised in any form or by any electronic, mechanical, or other means,
now known or hereafter invented, including photocopying and recording,
or in any information storage or retrieval system, without permission in
writing from the publishers.

Trademark notice: Product or corporate names may be trademarks or
registered trademarks, and are used only for identification and
explanation without intent to infringe.

British Library Cataloguing in Publication Data
A catalogue record for this book is available from the British Library

ISBN 13: 978-1-138-56459-6

Typeset in Times New Roman
by RefineCatch Limited, Bungay, Suffolk

Publisher's Note
The publisher accepts responsibility for any inconsistencies that may have
arisen during the conversion of this book from journal articles to book chapters,
namely the possible inclusion of journal terminology.

Disclaimer
Every effort has been made to contact copyright holders for their permission to
reprint material in this book. The publishers would be grateful to hear from any
copyright holder who is not here acknowledged and will undertake to rectify
any errors or omissions in future editions of this book.

Contents

Citation Information   vii

Notes on Contributors   ix

1. Chinese-Foreign Cooperation in Running Schools   1
   Lin Jinhui

2. A Discussion on Improving the Quality of Sino-Foreign Cooperative Education   3
   Lin Jinhui and Liu Mengjin

3. Study on the Introduction of High-Quality Educational Resources for Sino-Foreign Cooperative Education   15
   Lin Jinhui

4. Basic Relationships Among Scale, Quality, and Benefits in Sino-Foreign Cooperative Education   26
   Lin Jinhui

5. Addressing Sustainable International Branch Campus Development Through an Organizational Structure Lens: A Comparative Analysis of China, Qatar, and the United Arab Emirates   43
   Jill Borgos

6. Hong Kong's Cross-System University Partnerships   60
   Gerard A. Postiglione, Qin Yunyun, and Alice Y.C. Te

7. Cross-Border Higher Education in China: How the Field of Research Has Developed   75
   Qin Yunyun and Alice Y.C. Te

8. Independent Chinese-Foreign Collaborative Universities and their Quest for Legitimacy   96
   Li Zhang and Kevin Kinser

Index   115

Citation Information

The chapters in this book were originally published in *Chinese Education & Society*, volume 49, issue 4–5 (July–October 2016). When citing this material, please use the original page numbering for each article, as follows:

Chapter 1
Chinese-Foreign Cooperation in Running Schools
Lin Jinhui
Chinese Education & Society, volume 49, issue 4–5 (July–October 2016), pp. 229–230

Chapter 2
A Discussion on Improving the Quality of Sino-Foreign Cooperative Education
Lin Jinhui and Liu Mengjin
Chinese Education & Society, volume 49, issue 4–5 (July–October 2016), pp. 231–242

Chapter 3
Study on the Introduction of High-Quality Educational Resources for Sino-Foreign Cooperative Education
Lin Jinhui
Chinese Education & Society, volume 49, issue 4–5 (July–October 2016), pp. 243–253

Chapter 4
Basic Relationships Among Scale, Quality, and Benefits in Sino-Foreign Cooperative Education
Lin Jinhui
Chinese Education & Society, volume 49, issue 4–5 (July–October 2016), pp. 254–270

Chapter 5
Addressing Sustainable International Branch Campus Development Through an Organizational Structure Lens: A Comparative Analysis of China, Qatar, and the United Arab Emirates
Jill Borgos
Chinese Education & Society, volume 49, issue 4–5 (July–October 2016), pp. 271–287

CITATION INFORMATION

Chapter 6

Hong Kong's Cross-System University Partnerships
Gerard A. Postiglione, Qin Yunyun, and Alice Y.C. Te
Chinese Education & Society, volume 49, issue 4–5 (July–October 2016), pp. 288–302

Chapter 7

Cross-Border Higher Education in China: How the Field of Research Has Developed
Qin Yunyun and Alice Y.C. Te
Chinese Education & Society, volume 49, issue 4–5 (July–October 2016), pp. 303–323

Chapter 8

Independent Chinese-Foreign Collaborative Universities and their Quest for Legitimacy
Li Zhang and Kevin Kinser
Chinese Education & Society, volume 49, issue 4–5 (July–October 2016), pp. 324–342

For any permission-related enquiries please visit:
http://www.tandfonline.com/page/help/permissions

Notes on Contributors

Jill Borgos is a Professor at SUNY Empire State College, USA.

Lin Jinhui is a Professor at Xiamen University, China. He is also Director of the Center of Research on Chinese-Foreign Cooperation in Running Schools (CRCFCRS).

Kevin Kinser is Professor of Education at Pennsylvania State College of Education, USA.

Liu Mengjin is a Postdoctoral Fellow at the University of Hong Kong.

Gerard A. Postiglione is Chair Professor in the Faculty of Education at the University of Hong Kong.

Alice Y.C. Te is a PhD student in the Division of Policy, Administration and Social Sciences Education at the University of Hong Kong.

Qin Yunyun is a PhD student in the Faculty of Education at the University of Hong Kong.

Li Zhang is a Project Manager for U.S.–Taiwan Partnership for International Research and Education (PIRE) at ASRC, University at Albany SUNY, USA.

Chinese-Foreign Cooperation in Running Schools

Lin Jinhui

Chinese-Foreign Cooperation in Running Schools (CFCRS) is one of the more than 10 forms of transnational education in China and the only one that China's State Council has issued regulations for. It is Regulations of the People's Republic of China on CFCRS issued in 2003. In the past 3 decades, CFCRS have been developing through four periods, including 1980–1995 (starting period), 1995–2003 (rapid growth), 2003–2010 (developing while adjusting), and 2010 to present (quality improvement period). That is to say, since July 2010, when the outline of the National Plan for Medium and Long-Term Education Reform and Development was issued and implemented, China has achieved great progress in both quantity and quality in CFCRS programs. By July 2016, 2,428 CFCRS institutions and programs had been approved by the Chinese government, among which 90% are in higher education. There are about 560,000 CFCRS students on campus nationwide, among whom 460,000 are in higher education, and the graduates have exceeded 1.6 million.

CFCRS is closely related to cross-border education. Statistics show that about 600 foreign partners in CFCRS programs are from more than 30 countries and regions. And the number of partners is continuing to grow. The reason is that CFCRS policy makers in China have realized the potential high-quality education resources are from different countries instead of just from several traditional education-exporting countries. So China proposed "the Belt and Road Initiatives" (B&R) by pushing countries to the west and southeast of China to establish an education cooperation community and to encourage high-level CFCRS programs in these countries.

If we want to focus on the quality and sustainable development of CFCRS, we should not only study CFCRS itself but also cross-border education in general. Therefore, in this issue of *Chinese Education and Society* my co–guest editor Kevin Kinser and I have selected seven articles in CFCRS and cross-border education. They provide information on the history and current situation of CFCRS to institutes, teachers, and researchers who are interested in CFCRS and help them explore more theories and practices in this field.

It is an outcome of cooperation among the Center for Research on Chinese-Foreign Cooperation in Running Schools at Xiamen University (CRCFCRS), Wah Ching Center of Research on Education in China of the University of Hong Kong, and the Cross-Border Education Research Team (C-BERT) at the State University of New York at Albany and the Center for the Study of Higher Education at Pennsylvania State University. CRCFCRS is the first institute in China that focuses on research on Chinese-Foreign cooperation in running schools. Xiamen University has been working together on CFCRS researches with some scholars such as Prof. Gerard A. Postiglione at the University of Hong Kong for 14 years and it has been going deeper. C-BERT at the University at Albany, State University of New York, where Prof. Kevin Kinser worked, is a world-known research platform for cross-border education and has many cooperative programs with Xiamen University and the University of Hong Kong. I'm convinced that our cooperation will continue now that Prof. Kinser has moved on to the Pennsylvania State University.

I'd like to thank editors and translators at *Chinese Education and Society* for their efforts to make it happen. My great thanks also go to Dr. Xie Ailei at the University of Hong Kong.

A Discussion on Improving the Quality of Sino-Foreign Cooperative Education

Lin Jinhui and Liu Mengjin

Abstract: Since the release and implementation of the Outline of the National Plan for Medium and Long-Term Education Reform and Development (2010–20), Sino-foreign cooperative education has achieved great progress, gradually entering a new phase of high-level model development. At the same time, the profound conflicts and issues accumulated over the years at existing Sino-foreign cooperative educational institutions and programs have yet to be resolved. Quality improvement has become a distinctive theme in the new phase of development for Sino-foreign cooperative education. It is necessary to bring forth new ideas in terms of the concept of quality and quality standards in Sino-foreign cooperative education commensurate with its new phase of development, endeavoring to establish a quality assurance system and corresponding operating mechanisms for Sino-foreign cooperative education that comply with international standards while retaining Chinese characteristics. In this article we focus on an exploration of four quality assurance mechanisms: the approval and access mechanism, the classified regulation mechanism, the evaluation and accreditation mechanism, and the penalization and withdrawal mechanism.

As of December 2015, China had a total of 2371 Sino-foreign cooperative educational institutions and programs established or hosted by approved organizations, with a total of approximately 560,000 enrolled students; the number of graduates from higher Sino-foreign cooperative education had already exceeded 1.6 million. After more than 30 years of development, Sino-foreign cooperative education has developed from a supplement to Chinese education (Former State Education Commission 1995) into a component part of Chinese education (State Council of the People's Republic of China 2003), becoming one of the primary means of achieving cross-border education in China (Lin and Liu 2010). The issues of implementing quality education, deepening comprehensive reforms, improving the quality of education, and building the China Dream of educational openness with increased internationalization have become major theoretical and practical questions.

English translation © 2016 Taylor & Francis, Inc. from the Chinese text "論中外合作辦學的質量建設" by Lin Jinhui and Liu Mengjin. Translated by Carissa Fletcher. Originally published in *Educational Research* (教育研究), 2013, (10).

IMPROVING QUALITY IS A DISTINCTIVE THEME IN THE NEW PHASE OF HIGH-LEVEL MODEL DEVELOPMENT FOR SINO-FOREIGN COOPERATIVE EDUCATION

The Common Appeal for Quality in Education Has Become an International Trend in Cross-Border Education

In reviewing the recent trends of international development in cross-border education, the concept of education has experienced a trend toward diversification. Conventionally, the countries providing cross-border education predominantly hold a view of education geared toward obtaining more economic benefits: for instance, the United States, Britain, Australia, New Zealand, and other typical education-exporting countries all treat cross-border education as their principal export industry, driven by the idea of gaining more trade volume for educational exports. However, following the continuous development of economic globalization and internationalization, a clearer trend toward diversification of the concept of cross-border education has been seen amongst the educational institutions of some countries, particularly the first-rate universities: the emphasis on international understanding, increased capacity building, development of human resources, and other concepts has left a deep impression. For instance, while New York University Shanghai, a model example of Sino-American cooperative education, has relatively high annual tuition (the 295 students admitted to the first class in 2013 included 150 mainland Chinese students, who paid annual tuition fees of 100,000 yuan, and 145 overseas students, who paid annual tuition fees of 45,000 USD), these sums are practically negligible compared to the funding support received by New York University in the United States, as such famous universities annually command up to several million USD in annual donations; in addition, schools engaging in overseas cooperative education face major challenges in preventing an impact to their reputation, et cetera, and must carefully and scientifically evaluate the risks. Duke University of the United States cooperated with Wuhan University and the Kunshan Municipal Government to establish Duke Kunshan University: in our analysis, as the foreign partner, Duke University "hoped to draw support from the progress of internationalization to remedy its regrets at having failed to beat Harvard on its home turf" (Lin 2013). according to a ranking of American universities published by *U.S. News & World Report* in 2016, Duke University ranks 8th (U.S. News & World Report 2016).

More and more international organizations are actively advocating for and promoting quality assurance in cross-border education, and have established various distinctive quality assurance models for cross-border education. Effectively guaranteeing students' interests has become one of the key focal points for each country. For instance, in 2005, the United Nations Educational, Scientific and Cultural Organization (UNESCO) and the Organization for Economic Cooperation and Development (OECD) jointly formulated the Guidelines for Quality Provision in Cross-Border Higher Education, which were aimed at supporting and encouraging international cooperation, and improving awareness of the importance of quality assurance in cross-border higher education; protecting students and other interested parties to prevent encroachment on their rights by inferior or nonstandard educators; and simultaneously encouraging the development of high-quality cross-border higher education that can satisfy social, economic, and cultural needs (UNESCO/OECD 2005). Some regional international organizations have also focused a high degree of attention on this matter. For instance, the European Network for Quality Assurance in Higher Education (ENQA) set the goal of promoting cooperation on quality assurance in higher education across Europe (ENQA 2013), and the

Standards and Guidelines for Quality Assurance in the European Higher Education Area drafted by ENQA were recently adopted at its Ministerial Meeting convened in Bologna (ENQA 2015). Many countries have successively formulated policies related to quality assurance in cross-border education: for instance, Australia proposed the Transnational Quality Strategy; and the U.K. Quality Assurance Agency for Higher Education (QAA) published the Code of Practice for the Assurance of Academic Quality and Standards in Higher Education: Collaborative Provision and Flexible and Distributed Learning (Including E-Learning). The cross-border education quality assurance models put forward by each country can be divided into two main categories, respectively represented by the United States and Australia. The educational quality accreditation system of the United States is a highly effective administrative system subsumed under its systems for division of power and educational diversification, while also serving as a type of quality assurance model for cross-border education. In comparison, Australia's quality assurance for cross-border education is characterized by government promotional efforts, through powerful policies, funding support and other leverage. Regardless of the model, the objective is to ensure quality and allow for the sustainable development of cross-border education.

Key Advances and Existing Problems in Improving the Quality of Sino-Foreign Cooperative Education

Quality is the lifeline of Sino-foreign cooperative education (Lin 2010). This was the thesis of a theoretical essay that was written for the *People's Daily* (Renmin ribao) of August 27, 2010 (Lin 2010). In the essay the author discusses the two fundamental patterns of Sino-foreign cooperative education, calling for Sino-foreign cooperative education to operate in accordance with educational patterns, and comply with the patterns of Sino-foreign cooperative education. In the process of reforming Sino-foreign cooperative education, we must answer a prerequisite question: what is the purpose of these reforms? It is to improve the quality of Sino-foreign cooperative education, and improve the quality of internationalized talent training. All reforms must ultimately implement improvements to the quality of talent training in order to achieve real results. With this understanding and this plan in mind, some reforms to Sino-foreign cooperative education can move forward in the direction of profound and comprehensive reforms. Otherwise, the so-called reforms and innovation of Sino-foreign cooperative education will turn down the wrong path. Without a clear concept and orientation for improving quality, such reforms and innovation may be beneficial to improving educational quality, may have no effect on improving educational quality, or may be detrimental to improving educational quality; it could also come at the cost of lowering the quality of talent training. The facts of the reform and development of Sino-foreign cooperative education over the last 10 or more years show that the above situations have all existed at one point or another.

In the five years since the release and implementation of the Outline of the National Plan for Medium and Long-Term Education Reform and Development (2010–20) (hereafter termed the Education Plan Outline), Sino-foreign cooperative education has experienced many new changes, has achieved new progress, and has gradually entered a new phase of high-level model development. During that five-year period, some Sino-foreign cooperative educational institutions and programs with a good educational foundation and relatively high starting point have gained approval, and have played a model role, and some high-level Sino-foreign cooperative education institutions and programs at colleges and universities under the 985 and 211 projects have also played a leading role in higher Sino-foreign cooperative education. Certain well-run institutions and programs have also served as a model example for mediocre or poorly-managed institutions and programs. From a regional perspective, Sino-foreign cooperative education in eastern regions has served as a guide for Sino-foreign cooperative education in western regions. In the course of 5 years, the top-down planning and quality oversight of Sino-foreign cooperative education have also reflected high-level model characteristics. The national education department has unveiled a cluster of major measures, sending a policy signal for the promotion of high-level model development for Sino-foreign cooperative education. For example, in March 2012, the Office of the Ministry of Education issued the Notice Regarding Strengthened Standards Management in Foreign-Affiliated Education (Office of the Ministry of Education of the People's Republic of China 2012), which required further clarification of the policy definition of Sino-foreign cooperative education. The ministry is currently engaged in intensive research to formulate the guiding recommendations for the administration of Sino-foreign cooperative education at the undergraduate level and the postgraduate level, as well as the guiding recommendations for quality assurance for Sino-foreign cooperative education at colleges and universities. In January 2013, on the foundation of experience summarized from the pilot evaluation of Sino-foreign cooperative education in three provinces (Jiangsu, Henan, Liaoning) and one municipality directly under the Central Government (Tianjin), the ministry initiated a new round of evaluations for Sino-foreign cooperative education.

Since the implementation of the Education Plan Outline, progress on Sino-foreign cooperative education has been of primary importance: the many real advantages that it brings to educators must be fully recognized. On the other hand, the profound conflicts and issues that have accumulated over the past 10 years or more at existing Sino-foreign cooperative educational institutions and programs have yet to be resolved. The overall standards and quality of introduced educational resources need improvement, and the educational practices at some institutions and programs need further standardization; the structure of disciplines and majors must be further optimized, and the regional distribution and the distribution of cooperating countries must be more balanced. Overall, support for improvements to the quality of Sino-foreign cooperative education is still fairly feeble, and some policies related to quality improvement are short-term; it is necessary to engage in comprehensive reform and development.

The above issues are the key problems that must be resolved in the process of improving the quality of Sino-foreign cooperative education. These problems have all arisen in the course of the development of Sino-foreign cooperative education: it is necessary to establish concepts and perspectives on development and utilize the means and methods of development to affect their resolution.

INNOVATING THE CONCEPT OF QUALITY IN SINO-FOREIGN COOPERATIVE EDUCATION TO SUIT THE NEW PHASE OF DEVELOPMENT

Establishing the Concept That Sino-Foreign Cooperative Education Is a Component Part of Chinese Education

Accurately positioning Sino-foreign cooperative education is a necessary prerequisite in improving the quality of Sino-foreign cooperative education. The Regulations of the People's

CHINESE-FOREIGN COOPERATION IN RUNNING SCHOOLS

Republic of China on Chinese-Foreign Cooperation in Running Schools, which was released by the State Council in 2003, point out that "Sino-foreign cooperative education … is a component part of Chinese education." This was a major breakthrough compared to the "Temporary Provisions on Chinese–Foreign Cooperation in Running Schools," issued in 1995 by the former State Education Commission, which declared that "Sino-foreign cooperative education … is a supplement to Chinese education." The current issue is that this position inscribed in regulatory documents has not been translated into a popular understanding and value judgement: miscomprehension and erroneous methods directly linked to the understanding of the position of Sino-foreign cooperative education are still universally evident in the ideas and actions of certain local education departments, educational institutions, students and parents, as well as some theorists and practitioners. If cooperative education is positioned as a component part or important component part of Chinese education (Lin 2011a), then certain written or unwritten regulations and obsolete concepts of quality incommensurate with the development of Sino-foreign cooperative education can no longer be regarded as rational: the understanding of Sino-foreign cooperative education held by certain local governments, schools and parents will also thereby achieve a fundamental transformation. Currently, many schools do not recognize Sino-foreign cooperative education at the level of the school's internationalization strategy, positioning cooperative education as a supplement to the school's other educational activities, treating it as a means of earning income, and turning the school into a platform for dumping inferior foreign educational resources; although some colleges and universities have written the concept of internationalization into the school development plan and strategy, they have failed to incorporate Sino-foreign cooperative education into the scope of management under the school's functional department for international cooperation and exchanges; some schools merely regard the function of international cooperation and exchanges as a foreign affairs department for entertaining visitors; some schools manage Sino-foreign cooperative education under the categories of adult education or continuing education, relaxing requirements for enrollment qualifications, pillaging the sources of students, and collecting high tuition fees, with chaotic management; still other schools simply use the approval documents for Sino-foreign cooperative education as a pretext for requesting permission from the pricing department to implement high fees. The above phenomena demonstrate that it is necessary to translate the position of cooperative education as provided in regulatory documents into conscious popular understanding and actions, to create a solid social foundation for improving the quality of Sino-foreign cooperative education. If the above problems cannot be fundamentally resolved, the efforts to improve the quality of Sino-foreign cooperative education will be no more than empty words.

Further clarification of the policy definition of Sino-foreign cooperative education will benefit the popular understanding of the position of Sino-foreign cooperative education, and establish a concept of quality in Sino-foreign cooperative education commensurate with its new phase of development. The entities involved in Sino-foreign cooperative education are Chinese and foreign educational institutions; the method is cooperation; and the primary audience is mainland Chinese citizens. Chinese educational institutions have not substantively introduced foreign educational resources, instead using the method of reciprocal credit recognition to engage in education and teaching activities with foreign educational institutions: for instance, ordinary intercollegiate exchange programs, study abroad preparatory courses, and the unilateral introduction of courses from some foreign educational institutions do not qualify as Sino-foreign cooperative education. At present, there are some individuals waving the banner of Sino-foreign cooperative education while engaging in activities that cannot be categorized as Sino-foreign cooperative education; others have intentionally or unintentionally blurred the policy definition of Sino-foreign cooperative education, imputing the problems that emerge in ordinary exchange activities to Sino-foreign cooperative education. All of the above are detrimental to improving the quality of Sino-foreign cooperative education.

Establishing a Correct Concept of Quality in Sino-Foreign Cooperative Education

It is necessary to have an objective formulation for quality in Sino-foreign cooperative education. In terms of the traditional concept of quality knowledge, the overall standards and quality of the foreign educational resources currently being introduced for Sino-foreign cooperative education tend to be low, and the quality of the students and teachers is generally low as well. However, if quality is evaluated under a different standard, the Sino-foreign cooperative educational institutions and programs are not all low-quality. What is educational quality? Quality in Sino-foreign cooperative education means having international vision, being proficient in international standards, being able to participate in international affairs and international competition, being able to fully exercise the talents of individuals, comporting with the needs of social development, and allowing students to achieve clear improvements over their original level.

The Education Plan Outline clearly stipulates that we must adapt to the needs of national socioeconomic opening up, and cultivate a large cohort of internationalized talents who have international vision, are proficient in international standards, and are able to participate in international affairs and international competition (State Council of People's Republic of China 2003). To establish a correct concept of quality in Sino-foreign cooperative education, we must first keep an eye on reality. For instance, during the phase of the massification of higher education, the conventional, purely academic pursuits of the past were no longer able to achieve the purpose of improving the quality of higher education, and were unable to adapt to the needs of promoting modernization. Generally speaking, during the phase of elite higher education, people focused on academic talent; and in the phase of massification of higher education, the talent market has more demand for professional talent (Pan 2000). The state has encouraged the launch of Sino-foreign cooperative education in the disciplines, majors and fields needed domestically, revolving around the cultivation of the outward-oriented, complex and practical talents needed for national and local socioeconomic development. Therefore, we must liberate ourselves from the conventional ideas of elite education, and transform the traditional concept of academic quality. Secondly, it is necessary to clarify the subject of educational quality. Talent cultivation is the core of education, and the concept of educational quality must set out from students' daily learning experiences, must be based on building up students' experiences, and must attend to students' individual growth and development. The goal of Sino-foreign cooperative education is training internationalized talent, and for high-level internationalized talent, "the most important standard is creativity: allowing students to have a sense of creativity and problem awareness is more important than anything else" (Ji 2012). In its proper significance, the concept of quality in Sino-foreign cooperative education means being able to cultivate students' creative spirit and allow students to individually achieve personal development, in the cognitive, emotional and other areas.

We must remain committed to the diversification of the concept of quality in Sino-foreign cooperative education. Different quality standards should apply to Sino-foreign cooperative educational institutions and programs at different levels, with different educational goals and different social adaptations, and there should be differentiated treatment. The following discussion of classified regulation will also further address these issues.

CREATING SINO-FOREIGN COOPERATIVE EDUCATION QUALITY ASSURANCE MECHANISMS LINKED TO INTERNATIONAL STANDARDS, WITH CHINESE CHARACTERISTICS

In a philosophical sense, a mechanism is a factor that effects the transformation of a conflict: establishing and perfecting mechanisms means seeking the factors that will shift a conflict in a positive direction. Following the expansion of the opening and reforms of Chinese education and the development of the practice of Sino-foreign cooperative education, the legal system that has been established for Sino-foreign cooperative education is still incommensurate with the new trends in some respects, and urgently requires further improvement. On the legal side, as improvements to the quality of Sino-foreign cooperative education move forward in accordance with the law, it is even more important that a quality assurance system linked to international standards and featuring Chinese characteristics be established, along with its operating mechanisms. Before carrying out revisions to existing policies, laws and regulations, general regulations or policy documents should be unveiled at the right moment, to build quality assurance mechanisms for Sino-foreign cooperative education, achieve the integration of rigid laws and flexible policy measures, and guide and guarantee the sustainable development of Sino-foreign cooperative education in the high-level model direction.

Approval and Access Mechanisms

Quality assurance in Sino-foreign cooperative education should start at the source by strictly controlling the "entrance" and perfecting the access and approval mechanisms. China implements the "approval system" and "credential system" in Sino-foreign cooperative education. Beginning in 2010, after a nearly four-year suspension of administrative approvals for Sino-foreign cooperative education, the Ministry of Education resumed the approval process, which has now been normalized. We must strictly control the approval gateway, fully investigate the feasibility and necessity of proposed Sino-foreign cooperative educational institutions or programs, further clarify the standards for access, reasonably set the threshold for access, and establish a preliminary evaluation system for applying institutions and programs. We must also further perfect the leadership systems and mechanisms in approvals for Sino-foreign cooperative educational institutions and programs; promote the establishment of mechanisms by which provincial-level educational departments proactively review applying programs, where possible; further strengthen the sense of responsibility at provincial-level educational departments, and lower the threshold for responsibility; and adhere to the basic laws and characteristics of foreign affairs work in education. While steadily promoting scientific management in Sino-foreign cooperative education, educational departments must also strengthen their macroscopic vision and oversight of "entry-level" quality, keeping close tabs on the matters for which they are responsible.

Macroscopically, it is necessary to complete top-down planning, focusing on the overall arrangements for regional distribution, distribution of disciplines, selection of exporting countries for educational resources, the ratio of institutions to programs, and other aspects of Sino-foreign cooperative education. At the microscopic level, we must strengthen the sense of responsibility among educating entities, and fully consider the needs of national and local socioeconomic development; we must also rationally integrate all school resources and magnify distinguishing features on the basis of the reality of the educating entity. At the same time, we must also guarantee the ranking and standards of the foreign cooperating institutions, and fully exercise the role of education offices (groups) at overseas embassies and consulates, strengthening investigative research on the high-quality educational resources of the given country and promoting the establishment of systems for the provision of trending information, selecting reputable educational institutions with reliable quality as the targets for collaboration, and upholding the principle of introducing high-quality educational resources.

Classified Regulation Mechanism

Always using the same quality standards to evaluate the quality of Sino-foreign cooperative education will cause evaluators to overlook the individual differences of institutions and programs, making it difficult to form distinguishing educational features. Such a system would also make it difficult to grasp the key points of quality assurance, which is detrimental to improving the quality of Sino-foreign cooperative education. It is necessary to establish the idea of classified management, based on the feature of diversified quality standards for Sino-foreign cooperative education. From the perspective of the current situation, Sino-foreign cooperative education can primarily be divided into the two general categories of institutions and programs for differentiated management. Sino-foreign cooperative educational institutions can be further divided into institutions with legal entity and those without legal entity. Strong alliances with high-level universities should be emphasized and encouraged for independently established Sino-foreign cooperative educational institutions; for Sino-foreign cooperative educational institutions without legal entity set up within a college or university, the distinguishing educational features of the Chinese and foreign cooperating parties should be emphasized, and both parties should be encouraged and supported in exercising their advantages in terms of academic disciplines, to promote discipline-building at Chinese colleges and universities; for Sino-foreign cooperative education programs, greater emphasis should be placed on cooperation in the areas of advantaged majors and curriculum development.

We must guide research-style universities, teaching-style universities and vocational and technical schools and institutes in fully considering the evaluation standards for high-quality higher educational resources relative to their choices in Sino-foreign cooperative education, geared toward their particular development goals, position, and characteristics. In addition, there should also be different focal points in quality assurance for different disciplines and majors in Sino-foreign cooperative education. In surveying the current distribution of majors among Sino-foreign cooperative educational institutions, it is not difficult to see that science and engineering occupy the dominant position. This is because the principles and laws of science and engineering are universal, and do not change when crossing national borders. Compared to the humanities and social sciences, science and engineering also have higher requirements with regard to educational facilities, particularly laboratories, which should be treated as another focal point in the process of quality improvement. In contrast, since the humanities and social sciences involve different cultural traditions and ideologies, their importation must be handled with greater care. As of September 2013, there were 884 sponsored Sino-foreign cooperative educational programs at the undergraduate level and postgraduate level approved by the Ministry of Education. Among these programs, some urgently needed majors still accounted for a fairly low percentage: for instance, the major of International Law accounted for less than 1%, which is inadequate given the new situation of the demand for a large group of legal specialists proficient in international law following the national opening and reforms. The reinforced restructuring of disciplines and majors in Sino-foreign cooperative education is an important link in quality improvements.

In boosting the process of establishing mechanisms for classified regulation, we must also further strengthen the establishment of information platforms for Sino-foreign cooperative education regulation work and platforms for the work of issuing credentials and accreditation in Sino-foreign cooperative education, to mobilize the enthusiasm of all elements of society for participating in oversight.

Evaluation and Accreditation Mechanisms

Quality evaluations and accreditation in Sino-foreign cooperative education should operate in service of quality improvements. The evaluation work for completed pilot programs in Sino-foreign cooperative education can play a certain role in promoting improvements to quality, but the phenomena of formulaic and fraudulent practices still remain. On the basis of summarizing the experiences of pilot program evaluations, the new round of quality evaluation work for Sino-foreign cooperative education has already begun.

In terms of the evaluation type and cycles, the evaluations currently in effect examine the qualifications of Sino-foreign cooperative educational institutions and programs; in principle, periodical evaluations shall also be carried out based on the approved operating term and training cycles for Sino-foreign cooperative education. A qualification evaluation is an access mechanism with minimum standards, and is out of sync with the market demand for high-quality educational resources (Tang 2013). On the foundation of qualification evaluations, it is possible to test and explore top-notch evaluation mechanisms, to promote the establishment of high-level model Sino-foreign cooperative educational institutions and programs. In terms of the evaluating entities, the evaluation work for Sino-foreign cooperative education is centrally organized by the International Department of the Ministry of Education and concretely implemented by the China Academic Degrees & Graduate Education Development Center of the Ministry of Education, with each provincial-level education department making the specific arrangements. Diverse evaluators are also drawn in, forming a setup with joint participation by the government, society, experts, Sino-foreign cooperative educators, and students, which is certainly praiseworthy.

Quality evaluations for Sino-foreign cooperative education must play a substantive role in improving quality, and must fundamentally answer questions related to the purpose of the evaluations, subject of the evaluations, and agent of the evaluations (Lin 2011b). It is necessary

CHINESE-FOREIGN COOPERATION IN RUNNING SCHOOLS

to further optimize and perfect the system of quality standards and evaluation indices. In accordance with China's national condition, a government-led intermediary evaluation system could gradually be established, allowing evaluation entities to develop further as diverse intermediary organizations with public input, powerfully guaranteeing the objectivity and fairness of quality evaluations.

Education accreditation systems originated in the United States, as an expression of the unique American concept of voluntarism. American accreditation is "a peer-review process carried out by volunteers" that is "voluntary and non-governmental." Glidden in the West, accreditation has already become the most widely-applied method of external quality assurance in education (Sanyal and Martin 2007), and it has been applied in cross-border education as well. Cross-border education accreditation primarily appears in four forms: accreditation by the local country's accreditation organization, accreditation by a foreign country's accreditation organization, accreditation by a professional organization, and accreditation by a cross-border education accreditation organization. The governments of many developing countries or transitioning countries (such as the Eastern European countries) regard accreditation as an important tool for the state to control the implementation of cross-border education, uphold educational sovereignty in terms of school standards, curricula and the conferral of degrees, and ensure that educational development conforms to the given country's economic, political, cultural and social policy objectives. In these countries, accreditation is largely controlled by the state, with the government establishing an autonomous or semiautonomous organization to carry out accreditation of education programs and institutions in accordance with the law. The schools and universities that pass accreditation can obtain a formal operating license and issue degrees recognized by the state (Gu and Xu 2006).

At present, the accreditation work for Sino-foreign cooperative education is still in the initial and exploratory stage. We should draw on beneficial international experiences to: explore organizational structures and operating mechanisms for accreditation in Sino-foreign cooperative education; begin resolving the major, prerequisite, fundamental problems faced in quality accreditation for Sino-foreign cooperative education on the theoretical and operational levels; and develop a distinctive accreditation index system that is clearly differentiated from the evaluation index system for Sino-foreign cooperative education, as well as exercising the role of quality accreditation in establishing model Sino-foreign cooperative educational institutions and programs. In exploring quality accreditation mechanisms for Sino-foreign cooperative education, we must also uphold the principles of objectivity, neutrality, and non-profitability, to effectively establish the authoritativeness and brand effect of accreditation. This is the only way that accreditation organizations can play their proper role in improving the quality of Sino-foreign cooperative education.

Penalization and Withdrawal Mechanisms

In terms of the experiences of cross-border education, many education importing countries highly value the ability to guarantee the quality of cross-border education through sanctioning measures. For instance, in Singapore, cross-border education emerged in the form of private education. To strengthen oversight for this form of education, in 2009, the Singapore government passed the "Private Education Act" and the "Private Education Regulations," establishing the "Enhanced Registration Framework" (abbreviated as ERF), which required that all private educational institutions (including foreign educational institutions) register with the Council for Private Education prior to beginning operations. "It is an offence for any private educational institution or persons to advertise courses not approved by the Council for Private Education, or collect fees from students for such courses. If a private educational institution is found to have committed these offenses, its registration term may be shortened, or its registration may even be suspended or cancelled (Singapore Council for Private Education 2009)."

One important question that must be answered today is how to achieve survival of the fittest to balance and restructure the system of Sino-foreign cooperative education. In April 2007, the Ministry of Education proposed the establishment of enforcement and penalization mechanisms for Sino-foreign cooperative education (Ministry of Education of the People's Republic of China 2007). However, over the last few years, the conditions for implementing this requirement have not been optimistic. At present, it is necessary to strengthen research and exploration of a withdrawal mechanism, to gradually establish and perfect a mechanism for the withdrawal of low-quality Sino-foreign cooperative educational entities. While exploring a withdrawal mechanism, we must also strengthen the sense of responsibility among educational entities and perfect an accountability system. On the foundation of quality evaluations, and in accordance with the law, we must severely punish Sino-foreign cooperative educational institutions and programs operating in violation of regulations or harming the interests of teachers and students. Unqualified programs shall be instructed to carry out reforms within a set time period: if the reforms are superficial, or if the entity is still unqualified after the reforms, it shall make an orderly withdrawal in accordance with relevant procedures.

The establishment of a withdrawal mechanisms must be guaranteed by relevant policies, laws and regulations, and supported by relevant accompanying requirements. We must explore and establish procedures and regulations for the termination of Sino-foreign cooperative education programs, and provide rational guidance and clear specifications for their withdrawal, such as giving advance notice, providing an opportunity for a hearing, et cetera, to ensure that the withdrawal procedure is fair and transparent. We must also communicate with foreign parties and ensure that the principle of "withdrawal in the case of poor operations" is embodied in cooperative agreements, to avoid disputes. Finally, we must formulate practical and feasible policy measures to resolve the questions of degree conferrals for students and compensation for dismissed teachers, to ensure that the interests of students and teachers are not compromised.

In sum, the exploration and establishment of a mechanism for the withdrawal of low-quality Sino-foreign cooperative educational entities is one important means of improving the quality of Sino-foreign cooperative education. This is a brand-new and innovative effort in the sphere of oversight for Sino-foreign cooperative education. These explorations will play a positive and promotional role with regard to discipline-building at schools, the innovation of school administrative systems and mechanisms, and even comprehensive educational reforms.

REFERENCES

ENQA. 2013. ENQA in a nutshell. http://www.enqa.eu/index.php/about-enqa/enqa-in-a-nutshell/ (accessed June 28, 2016).
ENQA. 2015. Standards and guidelines for quality assurance in the European higher education area. http://www.enqa.eu/index.php/home/esg/ (accessed June 28, 2016).

CHINESE-FOREIGN COOPERATION IN RUNNING SCHOOLS

Former State Education Commission. 1995. Guojia jiaowei guanyu fabu 'Zhong-wai hezuo banxue zanxing guiding' de tongzhi" (Notice of the state education commission regarding the temporary provisions on Chinese–Foreign cooperation in running schools), http://www.zzjy.gov.cn/images/jyfw/jycx/wx/jyfg/jybgz/jyzw/zcfg/files/zz186.htm (accessed June 28, 2016).

Glidden, R. 1998, June 25. The contemporary context of accreditation: Challenges in a changing environment. Keynote Address for 2nd CHEA "Usefulness" Conference. http://www.chea.org/Events/Usefulness/98May/98_05Glidden.asp (accessed June 28, 2016).

Gu, J. X., and H. Xu. 2006. Kuaguo jiaoyu de zhiliang baozhang, renzheng he zige renke (Quality assurance, accreditation and recognition of qualifications in cross-border education). *Bijiao jiaoyu yanjiu (Comparative Education Review)*, (4).

Ji, B. C. 2012. Guojixing rencai biaozhun shi chuangxin er fei liuyang beijing (The standard for internationalized talent is creativity, not a background in study abroad), *Zhongxin wang* (ChinaNews.com), June 12, 2012, http://www.chinanews.com/edu/2012/06-12/3956751.shtml (accessed June 28, 2016).

Lin, J. H. 2010, August 27. Zhong-wai hezuo banxue de guifan, jiankang, youxu (Standards, health and order in Sino-foreign cooperative education). *Renmin ribao* (People's Daily).

Lin, J. H. 2011a. Guifan banxue, yifa guanli, cujin Zhong-wai hezuo banxue kechixue fazhan—'Zhong-wai hezuo banxue: guifan banxue, yifa guanli, cujin Zhong-wai hezuo banxue kechixue fazhan guoji xueshu yantaohui' kaimushi shang de jianghua (Standard operations and lawful management, promoting the sustainable development of Sino-foreign cooperative education: speech at the opening ceremony of the 'International Academic Symposium on Sino-Foreign Cooperative Education: Standard Operations and Lawful Management, Promoting the Sustainable Development of Sino-Foreign Cooperative Education). *Guoji gaodeng jiaoyu yanjiu (Studies in International Higher Education)*, (3).

Lin, J. H. 2011b, September 14. Pinggu yinggai shi yizhong fuwu (Evaluations should be a type of service). Renmin ribao (People's Daily).

Lin, J. H. 2013, March 15. Bieyang liuxue xuyao bieyang baohu—dui tigao Zhong-wai hezuo banxue zhiliang de sikao (A different type of study abroad requires a different type of protection—thoughts on improving the quality of Sino-foreign cooperative education), Zhongguo jiaoyu bao (China Education News).

Lin, J. H., and Z. P. Liu. 2010. *Gaodeng jiaoyu Zhong-wai hezuo banxue yanjiu (A study of Sino-foreign cooperative education in higher education)*. Guangzhou, China: Guangdong jiaoyu chubanshe.

Ministry of Education of the People's Republic of China. 2007. Jiaoyubu guanyu jinyibu guifan Zhong-wai hezuo banxue zhixu de tongzhi (Notice of the Ministry of Education regarding further standardization of procedures in Sino-foreign cooperative education). http://www.moe.edu.cn/publicfiles/business/htmlfiles/moe/moe_862/201005/87664.html (accessed June 28, 2016).

Office of the Ministry of Education of the People's Republic of China. 2012. Jiaoyubu bangongting guanyu jiaqiang shewai banxue guifan guanli de tongzhi (Notice of the Ministry of Education regarding strengthened standards management in foreign-affiliated education). http://www.moe.gov.cn/publicfiles/business/htmlfiles/moe/moe_861/201204/xxgk_133915.html (accessed June 28, 2016).

Pan, M. Y. 2000. Gaodeng jiaoyu dazhonghua de jiaoyu zhiliang guan (The concept of educational quality in the popularization of higher education). *Zhongguo gaojiao yanjiu (China Higher Education Research)*, (1).

Sanyal, B. C., and M. Martin. 2007. *Quality assurance and the role of accreditation: An overview*. New York: Palgrave Macmillan.

Singapore Council for Private Education. 2010. *Qiangzhixing qianghua zhuce jiagou (Enhanced Registration Framework) (ERF)*. http://www.cpe.gov.sg/cn/for-peis/erf/erf (accessed June 28, 2016).

State Council of the People's Republic of China. 2003. Zhonghua renmin gongheguo Zhong-wai hezuo banxue tiaoli (Regulations of the People's Republic of China on Chinese-Foreign Cooperation in Running Schools). http://www.gov.cn/gongbao/content/2003/content_62030.htm (accessed June 28, 2016).

Tang, Z. F. 2013. Woguo gaodeng jiaoyu Zhong-wai hezuo banxue zhiliang baozhang tixi jianshe yanjiu (Study of the establishment of a quality assurance system for Sino-foreign cooperative education in Chinese higher education). *Jiangsu gaojiao (Jiangsu Higher Education)*, (2).

U.S. News & World Report. 2016. National universities rankings. http://colleges.usnews.rankingsandreviews.com/best-colleges/rankings/national-universities?.int=9ff208 (accessed June 28, 2016).

UNESCO/OECD. 2005. Guidelines for quality provision in cross-border higher education. http://www.oecd.org/dataoecd/27/51/35779480.pdf (accessed June 28, 2016).

Study on the Introduction of High-Quality Educational Resources for Sino-Foreign Cooperative Education

Lin Jinhui

Abstract: In Sino-foreign cooperative education, high-quality introduced educational resources must benefit the growth and development of students, facilitate the school's capacity building and the improvement of overall educational standards, and promote national socioeconomic development. It is necessary to establish and perfect the various working mechanisms for Sino-foreign cooperative education, restructure the strategic distribution of high-quality introduced educational resources, formulate relevant policy measures, explore new paths for cooperative education, strengthen initiative in cooperative education, and establish central planning and coordinating mechanisms for high-quality introduced educational resources; at the same time, it is necessary to strengthen capital investment, build a good social environment and atmosphere, establish a high-quality corps of talent for Sino-foreign cooperative education, and reinforce theoretical research on Sino-foreign cooperative education.

Making education more open and engaging in multilevel educational exchanges and cooperation across broad fields are important means of increasing the internationalization of Chinese education. Sino-foreign cooperative education plays a positive role in promoting innovation in school administrative systems and mechanisms and the reform of talent training models, as well as furthering the establishment of high-level universities. High-quality introduced educational resources are the core of Sino-foreign cooperative education, and a deciding factor in its success (Lin 2010). However, from an overall perspective, the quantity and quality of foreign educational resources currently being introduced through Sino-foreign cooperative education are still, in some ways, incommensurate with the new demands that the national Opening and Reforms and the internationalization of education have placed on Sino-foreign cooperative education, as well as the new expectations that society has for Sino-foreign cooperative education.

To better introduce high-quality educational resources for Sino-foreign cooperative education, it is necessary to accurately grasp the connotations and characteristics of high-quality foreign educational resources, and the significance of Sino-foreign cooperative education,

---

English translation © 2016 Taylor & Francis, Inc. from the Chinese text "中外合作辦學中引進優質教育資源問題研究" by Lin Jinhui. Translated by Carissa Fletcher. Originally published in *Educational Research* (教育研究), 2012, (10).

adopting the introduction of top-quality educational resources as the highest standard in the evaluation of Sino-foreign cooperative education, and promoting a profound transformation in ideas, concepts and development strategies; establish administrative concepts for the complete process of rationally introducing and effectively utilizing high-quality educational resources, respecting objective rules, and proceeding in accordance with regulations (Lin 2012); as well as establishing and perfecting long-term mechanisms for introducing high-quality educational resources, and proactively constructing a support system to uphold the functioning of these mechanisms.

WHAT ARE THE HIGH-QUALITY FOREIGN EDUCATIONAL RESOURCES IN SINO-FOREIGN COOPERATIVE EDUCATION?

Connotations and Characteristics of High-Quality Foreign Educational Resources

High-quality foreign educational resources refer to education and teaching concepts, talent training models, curricula, teaching materials, teaching methods, educational administrative systems, qualified teachers, administrative teams, and quality assurance systems, and so on, with advanced standards and educational qualities, as well as certain leading advantages on a global scale. In the sphere of higher education, high-quality foreign educational resources generally appear in the form of disciplines and majors that are distinguished in some way or which are based on educational experience.

Introduced high-quality foreign educational resources are characterized by diversity, practicality, complementarity, and proceduralization: these characteristics reflect the integration of relativism and absolutism. In the actual process of administrative approval and supervision on Sino-foreign cooperative educational programs and institutions, these important characteristics should be firmly upheld. In the sphere of higher education, with regard to Sino-foreign cooperative education, we should focus on how to promote the founding of world-class universities as well as local, distinguished, high-quality universities in China, fully exercising the role of Sino-foreign cooperative education in the establishment of disciplines at institutes of higher education, the reform of talent training models, as well as the innovation of administrative systems and mechanisms in higher education.

Diversity

In the sphere of higher education, high-quality educational resources include not only first-class foreign universities and the foremost disciplines, but also distinguished majors and high-quality curricula at foreign institutions, as well as the excellent teachers associated with them. Comprehensive world university rankings can serve as one referential basis for determining the quality of educational resources. However, rankings are not the only option in terms of the standards for high-quality educational resources: for instance, a famous university may feature average disciplines or majors, whereas a university with average rankings may have one or several distinguished, influential or high-quality disciplines or majors. Overall, the educational resources of the developed Western countries are fairly advanced. Among the current foreign partners of Sino-foreign cooperative education, those stemming from the United States, Britain, Australia and other developed countries occupy the majority. We must shift away from the idea that only developed countries are advantaged, and boldly explore the possibility of introducing high-quality educational resources from semi-developed and developing countries. A survey study found that India, Thailand, Vietnam, Malaysia, the Philippines, Indonesia, Brazil, Argentina, Chile, South Africa, Egypt, and other countries also have a fair amount of high-quality educational resources that China could introduce and utilize. In selecting foreign educational resources, we cannot simply rely on the results of overseas accreditation, as such accreditations are merely the minimum criteria, and do not reflect a school's true educational quality and standards; different types of Chinese higher education institutions and regions with differing socioeconomic development also identify differently with high-quality foreign educational resources, and have diverse demands.

Practicality

Sino-foreign cooperative education introduces high-quality foreign educational resources first to improve the quality of education at domestic schools and establish a strong education system in China; and second to train internationalized talents and promote the internationalization of Chinese education. The standards for high-quality educational resources have changed along-side the changing needs of socioeconomic development. Revolving around national talent, major scientific and technological projects, and the implementation of the Outline of the National Plan for Medium and Long-Term Education Reform and Development (2010–20) (hereafter termed the Education Plan Outline), priority consideration must be given to Sino-foreign cooperative education falling under the Provisional Plan for the Training of Top-Notch Students in Fundamental Disciplines, the Plan for Outstanding Engineers, and the Plan for Outstanding Doctors and Legal Talents, as well as the disciplines and majors sorely needed in key fields for national and local socioeconomic development, and the fundamental research, cutting-edge technological fields, and strategic emerging industries that have been granted priority national support, with an emphasis on introducing high-quality educational resources closely associated with these fields.

Complementarity

High-quality introduced educational resources should be well matched to Chinese educational institutions, disciplines and majors. The strengths, standards and characteristics of Chinese educational institutions must be fully considered to effectively pair the educational resources of both sides, with complementary advantages. We must encourage and support Chinese educational institutions in carefully integrating the demands of national, regional and local socioeconomic development for various types of specialized personnel and the demands for the establishment of school disciplines and majors as well as a corps of qualified teachers in selecting high-quality educational that suit their own developmental needs, on the basis of their general position and development strategies. We must also encourage and support local undergraduate colleges and higher vocational institutions in cooperating with high-quality foreign education-based or education- and research-based universities and specialized institutions.

Proceduralization

The introduction of high-quality educational resources is a complete process that requires strengthened supervision (Chang and Shen 2012). First, it is necessary to strengthen communication and adjustment for both sides, and increase the enforceability of a Sino-Foreign Cooperative Education Agreement; second, it is necessary to make reference to the national state of affairs in carrying out indigenizing reforms of imported educational resources, engaging in absorption, assimilation, utilization, and innovation, to prevent a failure of acclimation for high-quality introduced educational resources, or even the phenomenon of high-quality educational resources sinking to average or inferior levels; third, it is necessary to adopt strong policy measures to urge Chinese educational institutions to mobilize and integrate the complementary advantages of existing high-quality educational resources and introduced educational resources, to transform the advantages of high-quality educational resources into educational characteristics and overall educational benefits for the school.

Three Key Points That Should Be Emphasized in the Introduction of High-Quality Educational Resources for Sino-Foreign Cooperative Education

Whether Sino-foreign cooperative education can become an important channel or "booster" for the internationalization of Chinese education ultimately depends on its ability to adapt to the requirements of national opening and reforms, and train a large batch of internationalized talents who have international vision, are well-versed in international regulations, and are able to participate in international affairs and international competition. The fundamental goal of education is to meet the needs of social development and comprehensive human development. In China's current stage of social development, people's value systems, society's demand for education, and the appeals that various interest groups make to Sino-foreign cooperative education are becoming diversified. It is necessary to increase the diversity and options of available education and continuously adapt to the public's new demands for Sino-foreign cooperative education by introducing high-quality educational resources.

Therefore, when introducing high-quality educational resources, it is necessary to emphasize three key points. The first is benefiting the growth and development of students. Education and teaching should be based on the patterns of students' physical and mental development, allowing each student to fully benefit from high-quality educational resources; they should also be student based and career oriented, and strongly uphold the legitimate interests of students in Sino-foreign cooperative educational institutions and programs. The second is benefiting the school's capacity building and the improvement of overall educational standards. The introduction of high-quality educational resources can drive innovation in the administrative systems, mechanisms and talent training models at Chinese schools, promoting the establishment of disciplines and curricula, and improving teacher quality. The third is benefiting national socioeconomic development, and promoting balanced and harmonious regional development. The high-quality educational resources introduced by Sino-foreign cooperative education must actively adapt to and serve the big picture of national reform and development. With regard to local colleges, when introducing high-quality educational resources, additional planning and management are required, according to the needs of local socioeconomic development. National educational administration departments should also set out from the principle of promoting balanced and harmonious regional development to strengthen macroscopic guidance and management for Sino-foreign cooperative education at local institutions, strictly upholding the quality of "imports" and education.

ESTABLISHING GUARANTEE MEASURES FOR THE INTRODUCTION OF HIGH-QUALITY EDUCATIONAL RESOURCES

Establishing and Perfecting Various Working Mechanisms for Sino-Foreign Cooperative Education

Since the issuance and implementation of the Education Plan Outline, enthusiasm for Sino-foreign cooperative education has surged at higher education institutions across the country, and the number of applications for Sino-foreign cooperative educational institutions and programs is continuously rising. At present, it is necessary to establish mechanisms for the preliminary evaluation and investigation of applying institution and programs, strictly controlling access, rigorously investigating Chinese schools intending to host (establish) Sino-foreign cooperative education programs (institutions), urging them to integrate related school resources, completing top-down designs for institutions or programs, and rationalizing the relationships between schools, institutions and programs, and other connections. If educational entities attempting to establish a new application for a Sino-foreign cooperative education program are already hosting another program, they shall be required to add a summary report of the existing program to the application materials for the new program. Educational entities' sense of responsibility should be strengthened, and the threshold for access to foreign educational resources should be appropriately raised. Provincial governments and their educational administration departments should reinforce organization and guidance for Sino-foreign cooperative education application work; streamline the relationship between the administrative duties of national- and provincial-level education departments, and the relationship between education departments and educators; encourage provincial-level education departments to actively review the programs under application, and review the establishment of mechanisms where possible; and urge them to carefully and rigorously review and inspect the application documents for Sino-foreign cooperative educational institutions and programs in their respective regions. We must focus on resolving the difficulties and problems faced by each province in reviewing projects and each local area in controlling standards; and as a pilot attempt, the item of "Social Stability Risk Evaluation for Intent to Host (Establish) a Sino-Foreign Cooperative Education Program (Institution)" may be added to application documents, requiring that Sino-foreign cooperative educators consciously assume responsibility for upholding social stability. The procedures for renewing and reviewing expiring Sino-foreign cooperative education programs can also be simplified on the foundation of quality assessment.

Restructuring the Strategic Distribution of High-Quality Introduced Educational Resources

Talent training has both periodicity and hysteresis, and it is necessary to take a long-term view in planning the distribution of disciplines and majors as well as the regional distribution of high-quality educational resources introduced by Sino-foreign cooperative education, providing principled guidelines from a strategic vantage point with regard to the focus for encouraging, limiting or banning certain disciplines and majors in cooperative education; provincial-level and local governments shall also be required to create focused mid- to long-term plans for the introduction of disciplines and majors, on the basis of the guiding principles. Dynamically adjusted mechanisms shall be established, and timely policy restructuring shall be implemented in accordance with the constantly changing and developing needs of education.

In terms of the regional distribution, planning should consider all aspects: improving the quality of Sino-foreign cooperative education in the Eastern coastal regions; coordinating with the Midwestern Educational Revitalization Plan; and encouraging and supporting undeveloped Midwestern regions in introducing the high-quality educational resources sorely needed for local socioeconomic development. In terms of the distribution of higher education institutions, the promotion of higher education institutions from the 985 project shall set out from the level of national strategic needs and target the world's famous, preeminent research universities for the introduction of high-quality educational resources, exercising and protecting the initiative and enthusiasm of local colleges and universities for Sino-foreign cooperative education; encouraging and supporting local colleges and universities in closely integrating the needs of local socioeconomic development and introducing high-quality educational resources commensurate with their own development goals; and exercising the primary role that local institutions can play in promoting the elevation of educational fairness and quality as the focal points in the development of higher education. It is also necessary to engage in dynamic and strategic restructuring in areas such as the selection of the exporting countries for educational resources, the ratio between institutions and programs, and the distribution of disciplines and majors.

Adopting Policy Measures for Categorized Management and Ensuring the Introduction of Top-Quality Educational Resources

Categorized management of Sino-foreign cooperative education is in keeping with China's national situation and the reality of cooperative education, and facilitates the introduction of high-quality educational resources and disciplines. In fact, some educational institutions have an inadequate understanding of the legitimacy of acquiring an economic interest in Sino-foreign economic education and the relevant policy restrictions. Existing laws, regulations and policies provide unclear prescriptions with regard to the matter of for-profit Sino-foreign cooperative education and a reasonable return, and there have been difficulties with operation and standardization in the course of their execution; some regulations have failed to adapt to the requirements of the World Trade Organization and other international organizations, and are inconsistent with the commitments made by the Chinese government. In practice, it is necessary to quickly formulate policy measures for the categorized management of for-profit and nonprofit Sino-foreign cooperative education: we must consistently uphold the principle of applying identical quality standards for supervision, further clarify the administrative responsibilities of the Ministry of Education and local governments, strengthen oversight of for-profit programs, and make the nonprofit orientation of Sino-foreign cooperative education more explicit.

Perfecting Policy Measures, Innovating Educational Models, and Implementing a Going Global Development Strategic for Cooperative Education

The launch of Going Global cooperative education for higher education institutions is an important measure to strengthen China's voice in the global education system, increase the international fame and influence of Chinese education, and promote the internationalization of Chinese education; it also has important significance with regard to deepening the understanding that overseas educational institutions have for Chinese education, while also expanding China's understanding of overseas educational institutions and educational resources, and promoting the flow of more high-quality overseas educational resources into Sino-foreign cooperative education. This measure facilitates reciprocity between China and other countries with regard to academic records, degrees and credits, and quality accreditation systems, achieving a breakthrough in the efforts for greater acknowledgement of China's academic system on the part of the developed countries, thus promoting the all-round development of Sino-foreign cooperative education.

It is necessary to fully mine the advantages of China's educational characteristics and traditional culture, circulate and integrate existing high-quality domestic educational resources, perfect the Going Global policy measures, and innovate the Going Global model. At present, Going Global cooperative education falls outside the scope of Sino-foreign cooperative education as provided in the Regulations of the People's Republic of China on Chinese-Foreign Cooperation in Running Schools, and incorporating it into the legal framework of Sino-foreign cooperative education for standardized management has been difficult. We must quickly present guidelines for Going Global cooperative education in higher education, while proactively and prudently implementing the Going Global development strategy for Sino-foreign cooperative education. Going Global cooperative education touches on the issues of educational sovereignty, educational oversight, and foreign exchange control, and it is necessary to perfect the relevant policy environment. We must also strengthen the establishment of internationalized school curricula, as well as perfecting schools' internal administrative systems, assessment systems for curricula and teaching at overseas cooperative programs, and mechanisms for the recognition of academic records and degrees.

Establishing Coordination and Planning Mechanisms for the Introduction of High-Quality Educational Resources

We must further strengthen central planning, comprehensive coordination, and macroscopic management for introduced high-quality educational resources, exercising the government's role of macroscopic regulation and guidance in the process of introducing high-quality educational resources. It is also necessary to stimulate the enthusiasm of local governments, their educational departments and relevant educational institutions for introducing high-quality educational resources, strengthen oversight and responsibility on the part of provincial governments in the introduction of high-quality educational resources, promote the formation of a scientific model for handling contingencies and irregularities in school administration at a provincial level, and establish administrative systems and mechanisms that adapt to new trends in the introduction of high-quality educational resources. We must quickly formulate guidelines for Sino-foreign cooperative education at the high school stage as well as the stage of preschool education, and strengthen proactive guidance and scientific regulation of the regional distribution of Sino-foreign cooperative education.

In the practice of Sino-foreign cooperative education, there is still insufficient coordination and cooperation between departments and organizations in the fields of education, human affairs, pricing, civil affairs, banking, customs, and taxation, and the accompanying policies, laws and regulations still need improvement. Examples include issues with the process of review and approval for bringing in overseas teachers, multiple exit/entry visas, and the necessity of residing in China for long periods of time to teach, as well as domestic certification and approval for students at educational organizations to continue their education through study abroad, which simultaneously involve departments and organizations in the fields of education, public security, labor, and notarization. The use of foreign exchange payments for the salaries of foreign teachers and the introduction of overseas teaching materials, equipment, and software similarly involve departments and organizations in the fields of education, foreign exchange, culture, customs, and taxation, whereas the enforcement of accountability systems for the introduction of educational resources requires the joint efforts of education, organization and human affairs, supervisory and auditing departments. We must innovate the working models to strengthen communication and coordination between all relevant government departments and other related organizations in the introduction of high-quality educational resources, promote the establishment of mechanisms for regular multidepartment conferencing, and perfect the mechanisms for multilateral coordination, joint promotion and pooling of efforts in the introduction of high-quality educational resources.

STRENGTHENING THE ESTABLISHMENT OF SUPPORT SYSTEMS FOR THE INTRODUCTION OF HIGH-QUALITY EDUCATIONAL RESOURCES

The establishment and implementation of long-term mechanisms for the introduction of high-quality educational resources will depend on strong financial support, public support, support from talents, and theoretical support.

Increasing Capital Investment in Sino-Foreign Cooperative Education and Strengthening Financial Support for the Introduction of High-Quality Educational Resources

We must formulate relevant policies to limit the cut that educational entities take from the tuition fees for on-campus institutions and programs; increase the transparency of cost accounting in Sino-foreign cooperative education, using auditing, oversight, and other means to put an end to the phenomenon of squandering resources; and urge educational entities to implement capital investment in the given school's Sino-foreign cooperative education institutions and programs through school funding appropriations, public fund-raising, the establishment of foundations and other methods, to quickly initiate a Sino-Foreign Cooperative Education Key Support Program (Discipline, Major or Institution) Construction Project. We must also rapidly introduce an evaluation and selection process of national model institutions or programs for Sino-foreign cooperative education, fundamentally settle questions such as the intended audience and the content of model demonstrations, and grant fiscal funding support and policy preferences to model institutions or programs for Sino-foreign cooperative education; as well as actively communicating, consulting about and promoting the implementation of financial aid, preferential tax policies, and policies related to foreign exchange control aimed toward Sino-foreign cooperative education. The establishment of Sino-foreign cooperative education grant foundations by local governments should be actively promoted and supported, to provide incentives and financial aid for the importation of high-quality educational resources for Sino-foreign cooperative education in the given region.

Creating a Good Social Environment and Atmosphere, and Strengthening Public Support for High-Quality Introduced Educational Resources

Improving the social environment for the importation of high-quality educational resources for Sino-foreign cooperative education and forming a public atmosphere for the common promotion of their reasonable introduction and effective utilization are essential to the scientific introduction of high-quality educational resources. It is necessary to exercise the guiding role of public opinion, strengthen mainstream discourses, actively grasp the conversation on the introduction of high-quality educational resources, form an enthusiastic and healthy discursive system, and improve the timeliness, authoritativeness, credibility, and influence of guidance through public discourse, so as to transform mistaken views and misunderstanding of high-quality imported educational resources. Some local education departments and educational institutions have an inadequate sense of the importance and urgency of introducing high-quality educational resources: a variety of methods should be adopted to gradually improve the ability of local education departments to guide public opinion with regard to high-quality introduced educational resources. A general public popularization and publicity drive for Sino-foreign cooperative education should be launched via research institutions and the mass media, promoting publicity work for the ideas, measures and projects adopted by each location and each educational institution to introduce high-quality educational resources. Students' and parents' rights to know, rights to participate, and rights to oversee Sino-foreign cooperative education institutions and programs must be effectively guaranteed, and major national and local policy measures to expand efforts for the introduction of high-quality educational resources must be publicized in a timely manner; successful methods and experiences in the local introduction of high-quality educational resources must also be promptly publicized and popularized, in an endeavor to open up new prospects for the active introduction of high-quality educational resources.

Expanding Efforts to Establish a High-Quality Corps of Talent for Sino-Foreign Cooperative Education

The scientific introduction of high-quality educational resources must rely on a large group of administrative personnel and other specialized talents who have theoretical knowledge of the concepts of internationalized education and Sino-foreign cooperative education, understand the tasks and requirements of national and regional educational cooperation and exchanges, are familiar with overseas educational systems, have the capacity to handle the day-to-day administration and practical operations of Sino-foreign cooperative education, and can adapt to new trends in the demands for Sino-foreign cooperative education.

We must launch administrative personnel training work and establish a training system for Sino-foreign cooperative education. Education on the knowledge, skills and qualities associated with high-quality imported educational resources must be incorporated into training plans and teaching systems; and it will also be necessary to engage in theoretical and practical training for the relevant personnel in the education departments of each province, autonomous region, and direct-controlled municipality, the relevant personnel of the functional departments for international cooperation and exchange at Chinese educational institutions, as well as the actual workers in Sino-foreign cooperative education at relevant educational institutions. We must correct the mistaken view and treatment of Sino-foreign cooperative education as simply foreign affairs work, increase awareness, initiative and administrative proficiency among administrative personnel at every level, and promote the scientific introduction of high-quality educational resources. It is necessary to quickly formulate a Training Program for Administrative Personnel in Sino-Foreign Cooperative Education, and initiate the training work as soon as possible, to gradually forward the normalization and systematization of training work for administrative personnel in Sino-foreign cooperative education.

We must expand the efforts to support the training of high-quality, specialized talents in Sino-foreign cooperative education. For many years, Xiamen University has led the nation in training doctoral students and Master's students in the major of education, with a research focus of Sino-foreign cooperative education; several other universities and colleges have also launched work in this area, but overall, the requirements for practical development still have not been met. We should encourage and support the establishment of Studies in Sino-Foreign Cooperative Education as a new discipline, using specialized education as a means of training the specialized professionals needed in Sino-foreign cooperative education.

Boosting the Scientific Study of Sino-Foreign Cooperative Education, and Strengthening Theoretical Support for the Introduction of High-Quality Educational Resources

The scientific study of Sino-foreign cooperative education is the foundation for promoting the scientific development of Sino-foreign cooperative education, and its level of development is a significant indicator for the development of the cause of Sino-foreign cooperative education. The study of Sino-foreign cooperative education should primarily focus on major practical issues and actively serve policy making, to reverse the situation of "unusable and inadequate" research in this area. We must fully exercise the advantage of research institutions in the field of Sino-foreign cooperative education as a platform for training and fostering administrative personnel and specialized professionals in cooperative education, to provide specialized support for the importation of high-quality educational resources. We must also proactively guide and promote the consolidation of research efforts, to jointly investigate patterns, serve policy making, and innovate theories, to guide the practice-oriented work to plan and build a national academic organization for Sino-foreign cooperative education.

REFERENCES

Chang, H., and Y. X. Shen. 2012. Dewei guoji gaozhong xiang mu luanxiang congsheng, zhengling bu xing, zhuanjia jianyi jiaqiang quancheng jianguan (Chaos abounds in Dulwich International High School Project: government orders are disobeyed, experts recommending strengthening general oversight). http://society.people.com.cn/n/2012/0801/c1008-18644146.html (accessed June 23, 2016).

Lin, J. H. 2010, August 27. Zhongwai hezuo banxue de guifan, jiankang, youxu (Standards, health and order in Sino-foreign cooperative education). *Renmin ribao* (People's Daily).

Lin, J. H. 2012. Zhongwai hezuo banxue jiben guilü jiqi yunyong" (Fundamental patterns in Sino-foreign cooperative education and their applications). *Jiangsu gaojiao (Jiangsu Higher Education)*, (1).

Basic Relationships Among Scale, Quality, and Benefits in Sino-Foreign Cooperative Education

Lin Jinhui

Abstract: The basic relationships among scale, quality, and benefits in Sino-foreign cooperative education are key to the development of cooperative education. It is necessary to construct a theoretical framework for the basic relationships among scale, quality, and benefits in Sino-foreign cooperative education and analyze the questions faced in development, to actively recognize and adapt to the new normal of economic development and the new stage of development in Sino-foreign cooperative education. The theoretical framework for the basic relationships among scale, quality, and benefits in Sino-foreign cooperative education consists of an appropriate scale as the foundation, innovative quality as the key, and increased benefits as the goal. In applying these three basic relational theories, we must uphold five basic principles: finding a point of balance, clarifying policy limits, highlighting key points for development, controlling standards for access, and exploring differentiated permissions.

As of December 2015, China had a total of 2,371 Sino-foreign cooperative education institutions and programs established or hosted by organizations reviewed and approved at the national and local levels. Over the next few years, how will Sino-foreign cooperative education develop, and what path will it take? To analyze these questions, it is necessary to properly address the major relationships among scale, quality, and benefits in the development of Sino-foreign cooperative education.

THE PRACTICAL NECESSITY OF PROPERLY ADDRESSING THE BASIC RELATIONSHIPS AMONG SCALE, QUALITY, AND BENEFITS IN SINO-FOREIGN COOPERATIVE EDUCATION

The Moment for Addressing the Basic Relationships Among Scale, Quality, and Benefits in Sino-Foreign Cooperative Education Is Ripening

Sino-foreign cooperative education has experienced more than 30 years of development, and has already reached a relatively sizeable scale. Figure 1 shows the number of Sino-foreign

---

English translation © 2016 Taylor & Francis, Inc. from the Chinese text by Lin Jinhui. Translated by Carissa Fletcher. Color versions of one or more of the figures in this article can be found online at www.tandfonline.com/mced.

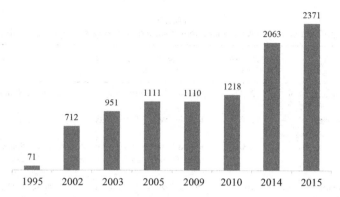

FIGURE 1 Diagram of the development of Sino-foreign cooperative educational institutions and programs by quantity.

cooperative educational institutions and programs from 1995 to 2015. At the same time, conflicts among scale, quality, and benefits have become increasingly apparent, and our understanding of the relationships between these three factors has gradually deepened. Properly addressing the basic relationships among scale, quality, and benefits has now become a real possibility.

Number of Institutions, Programs, and Students in Sino-Foreign Cooperative Education

At present, among the 2,371 Sino-foreign cooperative educational institutions and programs nationwide, there are 1,084 cooperative education programs at the undergraduate level and the postgraduate level, 11 higher education Sino-foreign cooperative educational institutions with entity status (including those in the planning stage, as shown in Table 1) and 57 Sino-foreign cooperative educational institutions without entity status (including those in the planning stage). Including higher vocational and higher technical Sino-foreign cooperative educational institutions and programs, the number of higher education institutions and programs for Sino-foreign cooperative education accounts for approximately 90% of all institutions and programs.

Since 2010, new approvals were granted to six Sino-foreign cooperative educational institutions in higher education with entity status (including two that have been approved for planning and establishment), and 26 Sino-foreign cooperative educational institutions without entity status (including one that has been approved for planning and establishment); as well as to 578 Sino-foreign cooperative education programs at the undergraduate level and the postgraduate level. The cumulative total for newly approved Sino-foreign cooperative educational institutions and programs at the undergraduate level and the postgraduate level is 610. In other words, over the course of five years, one Sino-foreign cooperative educational institution or program at the undergraduate level and the postgraduate level came into being every three days, on average.

As of December 2015, there were approximately 560,000 students enrolled in Sino-foreign cooperative education nationwide: this included approximately 460,000 students enrolled in Sino-foreign cooperative education in the higher education stage. The

CHINESE-FOREIGN COOPERATION IN RUNNING SCHOOLS

TABLE 1
List of Sino-foreign Cooperative Educational Institutions in Higher Education with Entity Status

Institution name	Approval date	Chinese cooperative party	Foreign cooperative party
Cheung Kong Graduate School of Business	2002	Shantou University	Li Ka Shing Foundation (Hong Kong)
University of Nottingham Ningbo	2004	Zhejiang Wanli University	University of Nottingham (UK)
HKU Space Global College Suzhou	2005	Suzhou University of Science and Technology	HKU Space, School of Professional and Continuing Education (Hong Kong)
Beijing Normal University-Hong Kong Baptist University United International College	2005	Beijing Normal University	Hong Kong Baptist University (Hong Kong)
Xi'an Jiaotong-Liverpool University	2006	Xi'an Jiaotong University	Liverpool University (UK)
New York University Shanghai	2011	East China Normal University	New York University (USA)
Duke Kunshan University	2011	Wuhan University	Duke University (USA)
Kean University-Wenzhou	2011	Wenzhou University	Kean University (USA)
The Chinese University of Hong Kong, Shenzhen	2012	Shenzhen University	The Chinese University of Hong Kong (Hong Kong)
Guangdong Technion-Israel Institute of Technology (Planned)	2015	Shantou University	Technion-Israel Institute of Technology (Israel)
Shenzhen BIT-MSU University (Planned)	2015	Beijing Institute of Technology	Moscow State University (Russia)

graduates from Sino-foreign cooperative education have already exceeded 1.6 million. Enrolled students at some Sino-foreign cooperative educational institutions number in the thousands, while some institutions and programs have only a few hundred enrolled students. Nationwide, annual admissions for Sino-foreign cooperative educational institutions and programs exceed 100,000.

Structure by Category for Sino-Foreign Cooperative Education

Sino-foreign cooperative education programs at the undergraduate level and the postgraduate level include 872 undergraduate education programs and bachelor's degree programs; 200 master's degree programs; and 12 doctoral degree programs. Figure 2 demonstrates the percentage of Sino-foreign cooperative education programs at different levels.

Regional Distribution of Sino-Foreign Cooperative Education and Distribution of Cooperating Countries (Regions)

As of December 2015, the higher education Sino-foreign cooperative educational institutions with entity status were distributed across Guangdong (five, including the Cheung Kong Graduate School of Business education program, which has now relocated to Beijing), Jiangsu

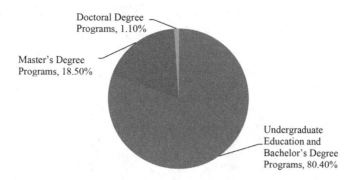

FIGURE 2 Diagram of Sino-foreign cooperative education by category. *Source*: Chinese-Foreign Cooperation in Running Schools.

(three), Zhejiang (two), and Shanghai (one). Sino-foreign cooperative educational institutions without entity status were distributed across 16 provinces and cities, including Shanghai (10), Liaoning (eight), Beijing (seven), Jiangsu (five), and Shandong (four), as shown in Figure 3. Figure 4 demonstrates the countries (regions) of origin of the overseas partner for institutions without entity status. The geographical distribution and countries (origins) of partnership institutions of Sino-foreign cooperative education programs at the undergraduate level and the postgraduate level are shown in Tables 2 and 3.

Distribution of Disciplines and Majors in Sino-Foreign Cooperative Education

As of December 2015, the nation's Sino-foreign cooperative educational institutions and programs involved 11 discipline categories. The disciplines included in Sino-foreign

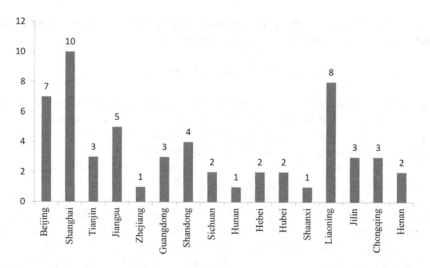

FIGURE 3 Quantitative distribution of Sino-foreign cooperative educational institutions without entity status.

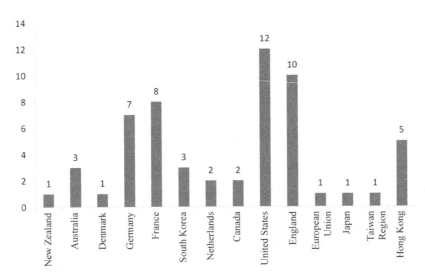

FIGURE 4 Distribution of the respective countries (regions) of foreign educational institutions cooperating with Sino-foreign cooperative educational institutions without entity status. *Source*: Chinese-Foreign Cooperation in Running Schools.

cooperative education programs at the undergraduate level and the postgraduate level are listed in Table 4.

As of December 2015, the foreign educational institutions cooperating in Sino-foreign cooperative educational institutions and programs stemmed from a total of 36 countries and regions. Among these, the classic education exporting countries were also the countries engaging the most in cooperative education with China.

The Urgency of Properly Addressing the Basic Relationships Among Scale, Quality, and Benefits in Sino-Foreign Cooperative Education

The Need to Actively Respond to Public Concerns

Sino-foreign cooperative education is currently attracting a high degree of public attention, and the focus of such attention is often related to the scale, quality, and benefits of Sino-foreign cooperative education. For instance, (1) Will improved quality and increased benefits for Sino-foreign cooperative education mean less development in terms of quantity? (2) What could be termed appropriate with regard to the overall scale and pace of development for Sino-foreign cooperative education? (3) How big must the scale of Sino-foreign cooperative education at a given higher education institution be to promote the internationalizing development of that institution? (4) What is an appropriate scale of admissions for Sino-foreign cooperative educational institutions and programs? (5) What is the likelihood that institutions planning or currently applying to establish or host a Sino-foreign cooperative educational institution or program will be approved? (6) After the Ministry of Education signaled that Sino-foreign cooperative educational institutions without entity status can be moderately developed, many

CHINESE-FOREIGN COOPERATION IN RUNNING SCHOOLS

TABLE 2
Quantitative Distribution of Sino-foreign Cooperative Education Programs at the Undergraduate Level and the Postgraduate Level

Province	n	%
Heilongjiang	176	16.2
Shanghai	109	10.1
Jiangsu	97	9.0
Beijing	96	8.9
Henan	82	7.6
Shandong	71	6.5
Zhejiang	60	5.5
Hubei	59	5.4
Jilin	42	3.9
Liaoning	37	3.4
Tianjin	35	3.2
Guangdong	25	2.3
Jiangxi	25	2.3
Hebei	23	2.1
Hunan	22	2.0
Chongqing	20	1.8
Total	1,084	
Fujian	17	1.6
Sichuan	16	1.5
Shaanxi	15	1.4
Anhui	14	1.3
Guangxi	14	1.3
Yunnan	10	0.9
Inner Mongolia	10	0.9
Guizhou	3	0.3
Shanxi	2	0.2
Hainan	2	0.2
Gansu	1	0.1
Xinjiang	1	0.1
Ningxia	0	0
Qinghai	0	0
Tibet	0	0
Total		100.0

Source: Chinese-Foreign Cooperation in Running Schools.

Chinese higher education institutions tested the water for the establishment of such institution; one Chinese higher education institution even applied for two Sino-foreign cooperative educational institutions in the space of one year. How high should the threshold be for Sino-foreign cooperative educational institutions without entity status? What should the application success rate be? (7) How can we overcome and eliminate the quality disorders encountered by Sino-foreign cooperative education in the course of development? (8) How should we understand and utilize the demonstration and radiation effects of Sino-foreign cooperative education in discipline-building and innovation of administrative systems and mechanisms at colleges and universities, to grant Sino-foreign cooperative educational institutions and programs their deserved place within school operations?

TABLE 3
Distribution of the Respective Countries (Regions) of Foreign Cooperating Institutions in Sino-foreign Cooperative Education at the Undergraduate Level and the Postgraduate Level

Country	n	%
England	243	22.4
United States	219	20.2
Australia	148	13.6
Russia	117	10.8
Canada	64	5.9
Germany	45	4.2
South Korea	44	4.0
France	41	3.8
Hong Kong	37	3.4
Ireland	31	2.8
New Zealand	18	1.6
Japan	13	1.2
The Netherlands	12	1.1
Italy	7	0.6
Sweden	7	0.6
Austria	4	0.4
Poland	4	0.4
Denmark	4	0.4
Taiwan	4	0.4
Singapore	4	0.4
Belgium	3	0.3
India	3	0.3
Belarus	2	0.2
Finland	2	0.2
Portugal	2	0.2
Ukraine	2	0.2
Spain	2	0.2
South Africa	1	0.1
Norway	1	0.1

Source: Chinese-Foreign Cooperation in Running Schools.

The Need to Actively Guide Public Opinion

The mainstream discourses on Sino-foreign cooperative education are imperfect, leaving parents and students perplexed by their choices, creating opportunities for rogue elements, and severely damaging the international image of Sino-foreign cooperative education as a part of multinational education. For instance, (1) due to a lack of common sense or driven by interests, harmful media outlets have released untruthful and false reports on Sino-foreign cooperative education, gravely impacting the social credibility and reputation of Sino-foreign cooperative education. (2) Some media outlets and websites have spontaneously provided critiques or rankings of Sino-foreign cooperative education, which have insufficient basis and distort public opinion, seriously disturbing the normal order of Sino-foreign cooperative education. (3) A number of institutions and programs have excessive admissions publicity, and some are leading people by the nose through dark intermediaries, severely misleading

TABLE 4
Distribution of Disciplines in Sino-foreign Cooperative Education Programs at the Undergraduate Level and the Postgraduate Level

Discipline	n	%
Engineering	398	36.7
Management	286	26.4
Economics	99	9.1
Art	83	7.6
Medicine	52	4.8
Science	43	4.0
Literature	42	4.0
Education	38	3.5
Agriculture	21	1.9
Law	21	1.9
History	1	0.1

Source: Chinese-Foreign Cooperation in Running Schools.

students and the public. We must look forward to creating a consensus in the sphere of Sino-foreign cooperative education. To prepare for the battle for discursive initiative and reverse the harmful tendencies and orientation of public opinion, it is necessary to engage in theoretical innovation and guidance with regard to the scale, quality, and benefits of Sino-foreign cooperative education.

TO PROPERLY ADDRESS THE BASIC RELATIONSHIPS AMONG SCALE, QUALITY, AND BENEFITS IN SINO-FOREIGN COOPERATIVE EDUCATION, IT IS NECESSARY TO HAVE A PRACTICABLE THEORETICAL FRAMEWORK

Basic relationships objectively exist among scale, quality, and benefits in Sino-foreign cooperative education. Properly addressing the basic relationships between the three factors also means correctly understanding and grasping these basic relationships, allowing the harmonious and sustainable development of the three elements.

To properly address the basic relationships between the three factors, it is necessary to have a practicable theoretical framework. The theoretical framework I propose regarding the basic relationships among scale, quality, and benefits in Sino-foreign cooperative education consists of an appropriate scale as the foundation, innovative quality as the key, and increased benefits as the goal.

Appropriate Scale as the Foundation

Unless a certain scale is reached, it is difficult to achieve quality or derive benefits. In 1995, there were only 71 Sino-foreign cooperative educational institutions nationwide (at the time, the program category did not exist), and it was difficult to form an economy of scale or a scale effect. This also applies to the scale of a single institution or program (i.e., the number of students admitted). If a given institution or program only has a handful of students, educational planning and organizing will both be very problematic, and quality will be a mere afterthought. Institution and program fees are determined by the local pricing department in conjunction with the education and finance departments, in accordance with the principle of compensation at cost, as well as appropriate consideration for the level of local economic development and students' ability to pay. Although some provinces have granted institutions and programs the power to autonomously determine and report their fees, if the fees are too high, students will compare the sums involved in deciding whether to study overseas or attend a Sino-foreign cooperative education program, and will vote with their feet. The importation of high-quality educational resources and qualified teachers is also key: as the saying goes, "Teachers are money!" Unless a certain threshold is reached for student admissions, even costs cannot be guaranteed, let alone quality and benefits. Conversely, attending to quality and benefits can also be difficult when the scale is too large, or development is overly rapid. If quality and benefits are not emphasized in a large-scale program, the negative effect of increasingly poor quality and benefits may emerge as the scale grows.

Research and planning are always worthwhile in an expansion of scale, even for a single institution or program. Many educational institutions have made the wise choice of being small but refined. The draft resolution for "Encouraging the Development of Small and Micro Schools" presented by Professor Zhu Yongxin, vice-chair of the Central Committee of the China Association for Promoting Democracy, at the 2015 Chinese People's Political Consultative Conference, has enlightening significance for Sino-foreign cooperative education (Zhu 2015). New York University Shanghai annually admits 300 students; Duke Kunshan University has also adopted the small but refined educational model. In the course of this survey study, we found that a Sino-foreign cooperative educational institution without entity status that has a total scale of 1,200 students and annually admits 300 students is fairly suitable. After a period of trial efforts, the Ministry of Education has established an authentication platform for the issuance of overseas transcripts and degree certificates in Sino-foreign cooperative education: 30 institutions and 456 programs have registered the degree certificate authentication information for a total of more than 100,000 students, and the platform has received more than 150,000 searches for various types of information, effectively containing the oversized admissions and other problems faced by some Sino-foreign cooperative educational institutions and programs.

The development of Sino-foreign cooperative education should be appropriately ahead of schedule, to ensure its colossal reputation. How to understand appropriately? First, it is necessary to occupy a lofty position, while also adhering to the laws of socioeconomic development and the basic patterns of Sino-foreign cooperative education, and conforming to the overall national situation of high-level educational opening and reforms; second, it is necessary to operate under requirements and conditions, based on the practical reality of the local government and higher education institution. *Ahead* means it is necessary to work ahead of schedule, due to the cyclical and delayed nature of talent training. We must fix our eyes on the future to achieve high-quality, beneficial growth and development.

Sino-foreign cooperative education currently still has space for development in terms of scale. From an overall perspective, policy innovation should focus on constantly creating new space for development, and establishing new mechanisms for stabilizing growth. The following few aspects are the focal points for growth and development.

CHINESE-FOREIGN COOPERATION IN RUNNING SCHOOLS

1. As of July 30, 2015, the total number of students enrolled in all categories of higher education nationwide had reached 35.59 million, and the gross enrollment ratio for higher education reached 37.5%. The Outline of the National Plan for Medium and Long-Term Education Reform and Development (2010–2020) stipulates that the gross enrollment ratio for higher education should reach 40% by 2020. In fact, based on the rate of increase seen in the gross enrollment ratio over the past few years, it may reach approximately 45% by 2020. The additional 5% will primarily be applied to restructuring in higher education, with expanded admissions for higher vocational and Sino-foreign cooperative education.

2. The gradual implementation and perfection of mechanisms for penalization and termination will allow the orderly withdrawal of certain Sino-foreign cooperative educational institutions and programs that fail to meet standards. The current focal points for policy are asset integration and a shift from an expansionist growth model to a balanced growth model. In January 2013, evaluations for Sino-foreign cooperative education entered the phase of normalizing development. In the 2013 round of evaluations, accreditation assessments were completed for 314 Sino-foreign cooperative educational institutions and programs at 129 universities and colleges across 23 provinces (cities), which were either nearing the expiration of their operating term, or had been approved for establishment or sponsoring by the Ministry of Education, including five institutions and 309 programs. In this round of evaluations, 88 projects (approximately one tenth of the total projects at the undergraduate level and the postgraduate level in the given year) withdrew from operation after failing to meet educational standards (including programs that failed their evaluation and those that voluntarily applied for nonparticipation in the evaluations, and stopped admitting students). Over the last few years, more than 100 Sino-foreign cooperative educational institutions and programs have been terminated through the evaluation process.

3. The scaling-up development of Sino-foreign cooperative education can also extend in the direction of overseas education. Sino-foreign cooperative education should incorporate "Bringing In" and "Going Global." Article 2 of the Regulations of the People's Republic of China on Chinese-Foreign Cooperation in Running Schools stipulates: "These regulations shall apply to educational institutions sponsored by foreign educational institutions in conjunction with Chinese educational institutions within Chinese territory, where Chinese citizens are the primary target of admissions" (State Council of the People's Republic of China 2003). This passage makes no reference to the direct definition for Sino-foreign cooperative education provided in the 1995 system of Temporary Provisions on Chinese–Foreign Cooperation in Running Schools, instead framing educational activities within certain parameters. The subtext of the prescription for the applicability of the regulations is that Sino-foreign cooperative education is a broad concept, and the Regulations only prescribe the standards for a portion of the educational activities it encompasses. I have previously proposed that overseas education be incorporated into the theoretical vision of and legal framework for Sino-foreign cooperative education (Lin and Liu 2008). Beginning in 2013, the Ministry of Education consolidated overseas education and Sino-foreign cooperative education under the same department for integrated management; certain

guidelines appearing in official documents have also expressed that overseas education falls under the framework of Sino-foreign cooperative education. The two aspects of Bringing In and Going Global are interlinked. As of December 2015, a total of 103 overseas educational institutions and programs nationwide had been approved by the authorizing organizations, including five institutions and 98 programs; these institutions and programs are distributed across 14 countries and regions. Overseas education is on the rise, and countries along the path of "the Belt and Road Initiatives" have a particularly exuberant demand for Going Global educational operations by Chinese colleges and universities, with a high volume of demand for cooperative education in the field of applied technical education. Some countries carry out full renovations of their school buildings before arriving to negotiate with Chinese colleges and universities and invite them to launch educational operations; this is known as "building a nest to attract a phoenix." The current policy trends for overseas education are: small but refined and programs first. One important bottleneck for overseas education is the shortage of bilingual faculties who can teach Chinese courses in a foreign language. We must begin planning as soon as possible, to provide resolutions in advance for questions related to disciplines, majors, and qualified teachers, et cetera.

Innovative Quality as the Key

Quality is the baseline guarantee for Sino-foreign cooperative education at scale. We must consolidate quality, while also engaging in innovation and improvements. This is the only means of achieving stable growth in scale and continuously increasing benefits. Quality is the fountainhead of benefits in Sino-foreign cooperative education, and the level of quality determines the extent to which the benefits of Sino-foreign cooperative education are exercised.

Recently, the Center of Research on Chinese-foreign Cooperation in Running Schools at Xiamen University completed the "Annual Report on Sino-Foreign Cooperative Education," a task commissioned by the Ministry of Education. The report found that the last few years of quality-building in Sino-foreign cooperative education have featured the following characteristics.

1. There has been a clear increase in high-quality Sino-foreign cooperative educational resources. Over the past few years, Sino-foreign educational institutions and programs with a good operational foundation and a high starting point have proliferated: the standing of the foreign cooperative educational institutions has risen to some extent, and the list of originating countries has expanded (the foreign educational institutions currently participating in Sino-foreign cooperative education stem from 36 countries and regions), drawing in high-quality educational resources from outside the typical education exporting countries. As of the present, more than 80 prestigious public higher education institutions from China's 985 project and 211 project are operating Sino-foreign cooperative education programs, accounting for nearly 20% of programs overall (a total of more than 600 Chinese

colleges and universities are participating in Sino-foreign cooperative education). Local colleges and universities are acting as the principal force in Sino-foreign cooperative education, operating a high number of programs with improving quality.

2. Quality assurance systems are continuously being perfected, and quality assurance mechanisms are increasingly being strengthened. The "Opinions of Further Strengthening Quality Assurance of Chinese-foreign Cooperation in Running Schools," which were issued by the Ministry of Education on December 10, 2013, are currently having an effect. A Sino-foreign cooperative education quality assurance system linked to international standards, with Chinese characteristics, is gradually taking shape. The internal governance structures for Sino-foreign cooperative education are undergoing continuous improvements. After more than 10 years of effective explorations, the board of directors of Sino-foreign cooperative universities is approaching perfection, and plays an important role in quality assurance. The level of development for internal governance structures at Sino-foreign cooperative educational institutions without entity status has also gradually improved. Subjective awareness of quality has clearly been strengthened at educational institutions and programs, and some institutions and programs have established model courses and refined courses in increasing numbers. Substantive cooperation with foreign institutions on courses, teaching materials, teaching, and qualified instructors is also constantly developing in depth and breadth.

3. High-quality, internationalized talent training systems have also gradually taken shape. The quality of Sino-foreign cooperative education is ultimately embodied in the quality of talent training. There are approximately 100,000 graduates from higher Sino-foreign cooperative education each year, and the employment rate has been rising year after year. The relevant data published by the Ministry of Education shows that the student employment rate at some Sino-foreign cooperative educational institutions is as high as 95% or more. Moreover, according to data from Jiangsu Province, in 2009–2014, the single institution and 34 programs in Jiangsu all qualified in the Ministry of Education evaluations for Sino-foreign cooperative educational institutions and programs at the undergraduate level and postgraduate level; and according to the tabulation of student appraisals and feedback information posted online, the satisfaction rate exceeded 90% for all program students, even reaching 98% for some (Yang, Jiang, and Zhang 2015). The number of students pursuing advanced studies at famous overseas universities after graduating from Sino-foreign cooperative educational institutions and programs has also climbed year after year.

On the other hand, while the number of Sino-foreign cooperative education operations has gradually increased over the past few years, quality issues are still relatively prominent. As noted in the "Opinions of Further Strengthening Quality Assurance of Chinese-foreign Cooperation in Running Schools": "A few higher education institutions have problems such as improper educational goals, a unilateral inclination toward the pursuit of profits, and low educational quality overall." As Sino-foreign cooperative education has grown in scale, more prominent quality problems have emerged.

Increased Benefits as the Goal

The amount of benefits derived from Sino-foreign cooperative education reflects the overall level of the educational operation. Continuously improving benefits are a sign that the Sino-foreign cooperative education has flourishing prospects. Conversely, if the benefits decline, Sino-foreign cooperative education will be unable to operate normally or continue developing. Unless a certain quality of development is met, it will be difficult to exercise the benefits of Sino-foreign cooperative education, whereas increased benefits will facilitate the promotion of expansion of scale and improved quality.

The benefits of Sino-foreign cooperative education are influenced by the scale and quality of the operation, as well as by the development outlook of the administrators and educators. In terms of the economic benefits and short-term benefits, the larger the scale, the greater the benefits; yet quality and benefits differ, in that ensuring quality may cause a decline in the economic benefits and short-term benefits, while sacrificing quality could bring about relatively good economic benefits and short-term benefits. This is the fundamental reason why some institutions disregard quality. Sino-foreign cooperative education must not only consider the economic benefits and short-term benefits, but also must emphasize the social benefits and long-term benefits. As a publicly beneficial undertaking, Sino-foreign cooperative education must place weight upon social benefits and long-term benefits.

With regard to social benefits and long-term benefits, the benefits of Sino-foreign cooperative education primarily manifest in the following:

1. Training high-quality, internationalized talents, to serve national and local socioeconomic development. This is also generally referred to as the contribution of Sino-foreign cooperative education.
2. Promoting discipline building in Chinese higher education institutions. In this regard, some colleges and universities have frequently encountered difficulties in deciding which discipline or major to select for cooperative education. Chinese higher education institutions generally choose an advantaged discipline or major, to combine their strength with foreign colleges and universities, and fully exercise the driving role of Sino-foreign cooperative education in building up disciplines; this is fairly easy to understand. However, some colleges and universities select a weak discipline or newly established major for cooperative education: the arguments presented in their applications stress that cooperative education can promote the development of disadvantaged disciplines or majors by leaps and bounds, to accelerate the progress of discipline building. Where the basic educational requirements have been met, this argument is sometimes granted consideration by the review group reviewing programs applications.
3. Promoting the innovation of educational administrative systems and mechanisms. For any university, when negotiating cooperation with foreign educational institutions, the first consideration should be the radiating effect that this institution or program can have on the other colleges at the school once it is successfully established. In other words, once the Sino-foreign cooperative education is in place, how will it benefit the teachers and students at other schools, and play a driving role in reforming the schools' overall administrative systems, education, and teaching. Several

Sino-foreign cooperative universities have already provided fresh experiences for system building at Chinese colleges and universities in terms of innovating the modern university system.

4. Satisfying society's diverse educational needs. When the people have money in their hands, the first thing they want to do is give their children a high-quality education. The primary channels for getting a high-quality foreign education are study abroad and Sino-foreign cooperative education. When Sino-foreign cooperative education was first developing, people referred to it as study abroad without leaving the country. Now the Ministry of Education intends to revive this slogan, and endow it with a new, timely significance. A survey of Jiangsu Province shows that 40% of parents hope to achieve their children's dream of going abroad by means of Sino-foreign cooperative education. This option occupied the highest percentage in the survey; 26.67% selected the option of a conventional study abroad intermediary organization. The surveyed parents expressed that the fact that Sino-foreign cooperative education is backed by a Chinese school is one of the primary factors for consideration in their selection (Wang 2015). On October 12, 2015, British newspaper *The Guardian* reported that "more Chinese entrants to English higher education institutions started their first degree through a transnational education pathway (55%) in 2013–14 than through direct student recruitment (36%), according to a recent report from the Higher Education Funding Council for England" (Choudaha 2015). It is clear that Sino-foreign cooperative education and overseas study go hand in hand.

APPLYING THE THEORETICAL FRAMEWORK FOR THE BASIC RELATIONSHIPS AMONG SCALE, QUALITY, AND BENEFITS IN SINO-FOREIGN COOPERATIVE EDUCATION

The conceptualization of the theoretical framework for the basic relationships among scale, quality, and benefits in Sino-foreign cooperative education is in the preliminary stage: it must be applied in practice and tested, with constant practical revisions and improvements.

In applying the theoretical framework for the basic relationships among scale, quality, and benefits in Sino-foreign cooperative education, the following five basic principles should be upheld.

The Principle of Finding a Point of Balance

In comprehensively planning out the basic relationships among scale, quality, and benefits in Sino-foreign cooperative education, it is necessary to find a point of balance at which the three factors can develop harmoniously. This point of balance will satisfy the people's growing demand for internationalized education, while upholding students' lawful rights and interests, in accordance with the law. To speak plainly, this principle involves figuring out the purpose of Sino-foreign cooperative education. Sino-foreign cooperative education concerns the fundamental interests of the people, and its fundamental purpose is to satisfy the people's growing demand for high-quality education. Upholding students' lawful rights and interests is both the starting point and ending point in planning out scale, quality, and benefits.

The Principle of Clarifying Policy Limits

Sino-foreign cooperative education implements both the approval system and the credential system: from the perspective of laws and policy systems, the policy limits are very clear-cut. The many problems that have emerged in Sino-foreign cooperative education have been related to an unclear understanding or intentional misreading of the policy limits on Sino-foreign cooperative education. The research report by the Center of Research on Chinese-foreign Cooperation in Running Schools at Xiamen University shows that there are 16 categories of foreign-affiliated Chinese educational operations, of which the category of Sino-foreign cooperative education has the most complete legal and policy systems and the most obvious social benefits: it is labeled by some as an in-system form of education, and it is listed alongside state-run schools and private schools as one element of the "troika" promoting the reform and development of Chinese education. Precisely because such a halo has been bestowed upon Sino-foreign cooperative education, some people intentionally blur the lines by, for instance, glorifying an ordinary intercollegiate exchange program with the name of "a new form of Sino-foreign cooperative education." When problems emerge in study-abroad preparatory courses, reciprocal recognition of course credits, and intercollegiate exchange programs, some people impute this bad reputation to Sino-foreign cooperative education. In addition, in reviewing applications for Sino-foreign cooperative education programs and secondary school institutions, the Sino-foreign cooperative education expert review group often finds that some Chinese educational institutions and foreign educational institutions conflate ordinary foreign-affiliated educational activities with Sino-foreign cooperative education when signing cooperative education agreements or designing talent training programs, applying for Sino-foreign cooperative education in the name of an intercollegiate exchange program: in such cases, the Chinese and foreign institutions are not engaged in any substantive cooperation, and the program for which they are applying amounts to reciprocal credit recognition or joint courses, at best.

The Principle of Highlighting Key Points for Development

It is necessary to promptly and accurately grasp the trends of development regarding the scale, quality, and benefits of Sino-foreign cooperative education, and closely pay attention to changes in society's demands or the source of students, et cetera. In recent years, the policy focus has been support for cooperative education in the fields of science, engineering, agriculture and medicine, as well as vital, weak or nonexistent disciplines. Strict controls are applied to cooperative education that has already reached a certain scale in the fields of business, administration, or disciplines controlled and assigned by the state. Energy conservation and environmental protection, high-end equipment manufacturing, atmospheric science, disaster nursing, ecology (natural resource conservation), water supply and drainage engineering, occupational therapy, physical therapy, ship-building and marine engineering, artificial limbs and orthopedics, cultural heritage conservation, interactive creativity, and other fields will continue to be encouraged majors for cooperative education over the next few years. In terms of policy orientation, for foreign educational institutions at an average educational level, strict controls will be applied where the same foreign educational institution is operating multiple cooperative education programs in China or intends to sponsor a fairly concentrated major. Encouragement and support will also be granted to higher vocational institutes and schools that are exploring the importation of refined or distinguished overseas vocational education and are focusing on training highly technical talents oriented toward the advanced manufacturing, modern agriculture, and modern service industries.

The Principle of Controlling Standards for Access

In comprehensively planning scale, quality, and benefits, it is necessary to clarify and uphold standards for access to Sino-foreign cooperative education, including the threshold of access for Chinese educational institutions and foreign educational institutions, as well as the standards for approval of Sino-foreign cooperative education. Only by upholding standards can growth be stabilized, and quality and benefits be ensured. It is necessary to exercise the guiding role that standards can play with regard to quality and benefits.

At present, several provinces and cities have adopted the general method of referring to various college rankings and proposing university cooperation with those ranked in the top several hundred around the world. This is a methodless method. In selecting a foreign partner, it is also necessary to comprehensively consider the ranking of its disciplines and majors, in accordance with the new requirement of establishing world-class universities and first-rate disciplines. The liberal arts colleges of the United States have educated many scientists and presidents, but they are not ranked at the top. The author believes that the qualification standards for foreign universities to engage in cooperation in China should be researched and formulated on an individual basis, according to the reality of Sino-foreign cooperative education.

Sino-foreign cooperative education is not McDonald's. The phenomenon of chain stores arose due to historical reasons in the early stages of Sino-foreign cooperative education, but in the new phase of quality building, this phenomenon no longer suits the times. At present, there are more than 300 foreign colleges and universities participating in Sino-foreign cooperative education, among which some universities are cooperating with Chinese universities to operate as many as several dozen Sino-foreign cooperative education programs: for instance, one Australian university has 44 cooperative education programs in China. Notices by relevant departments have pointed out that some foreign educational institutions are using Sino-foreign cooperative education to run profit-seeking chain stores. Some foreign institutions are operating multiple programs with different Chinese institutions for the same major, or are operating different programs with multiple Chinese institutions; still others are simultaneously operating multiple programs at the undergraduate and junior college levels. The objective of such education programs is to expand in quantity, and in essence, they amount to the dumping of foreign education: they cannot guarantee the importation of high-quality educational resources, and do not promote improvements to educational quality and standards. The Ministry of Education has already adopted measures to firmly restrain and gradually eliminate the "chain store" phenomenon: for instance, in applications for new programs, a red line will be drawn for the number of programs operated by a given foreign education institution in the same major, as well as for the number of institutions engaged in cooperative education alongside Chinese colleges and universities.

The Principle of Exploring Differentiated Permissions

To allow the overall arrangements and master plan for Sino-foreign cooperative education to take root, we must combine comprehensive planning with giving free rein to the initiative and creativity of different local governments and higher education institutions, encouraging and permitting them to engage in differentiated exploration, to resolve problems with impetus for development and the assumption of responsibility. Trial and error should also be permitted, with tolerance for failure. Scaled-up development, improved quality and increased benefits are all well and good, but distinguishing features are indispensable in Sino-foreign cooperative education. The method adopted by some local government and higher education institution of placing education with distinguishing features in the development plan for Sino-foreign cooperative education is well worth encouraging. At present, distinguishing features is one item in the evaluative index system for Sino-foreign cooperative education, but it is hard to evaluate. The addition of a few optional distinguishing features to the evaluations is an important issue that should be resolved in the course of establishing the evaluative system for Sino-foreign cooperative education. The development of Sino-foreign cooperative education has been relatively slow in some provinces and at some schools: for instances, Fujian Province is a liberal Eastern coastal province, a free trade zone and a core area for the Belt and Road Initiatives, but its Sino-foreign cooperative education programs account for less than 3% of the national total, and its higher education Sino-foreign cooperative educational institutions are currently at zero. In planning out and addressing scale, quality, and benefits, such provinces should be granted greater policy preferences and autonomy. In a reflection of this point, Fujian has become the second province nationwide to institute a pilot program for the ministry-province joint approval mechanism for Sino-foreign cooperative education.

REFERENCES

Chinese-Foreign Cooperation in Running Schools. 2016. Foreign-affiliated education oversight portal of the Ministry of Education. http://www.crs.jsj.edu.cn/index.php/default/index (accessed June 24, 2016).

Choudaha, R. 2015, October 12. How China plans to become a global force in higher education. *The Guardian*. http://www.theguardian.com/higher-education-network/2015/oct/12/how-china-plans-to-become-a-global-force-in-higher-education (accessed on June 24, 2016).

Lin, J. H., and Z. P. Liu. 2008. Gaodeng jiaoyu Zhong-wai hezuo banxue 'Zou chuqu' fazhan zhanlüe tanxin (Exploration of the 'Go Global' development strategy for Sino-foreign cooperative education in higher education). *Jiaoyu yanjiu (Education Research)*, (1).

State Council of the People's Republic of China. 2003. Regulations of the people's Republic of China on Chinese-Foreign cooperation in running schools. http://www.gov.cn/gongbao/content/2003/content_62030.htm (accessed June 24, 2016).

Wang, S. 2015, September 29. Haiwai liuxue 'wangyue' lailin, sicheng jiazhang qinglai Zhong-wai hezuo banxue (The 'peak month' for study abroad is approaching: forty percent of parents favor Sino-foreign cooperative education). *Changzhou wanbao* (Changzhou Evening News). http://www.gol.edu.cn/service_12685/20150929/t20150929_1001786.shtml (accessed June 24, 2016).

Yang, P. P., T. Y. Jiang, and X. Zhang. 2015, October 13. Jiangsu sheng Zhong-wai hezuo banxue chuang sige 'zui' (Sino-foreign cooperative education in Jiangsu Province sets four 'bests'). *Xinhua ribao* (Xinhua Daily). http://news.sina.com.cn/c/2015-10-14/doc-ifxiuyea9075540.shtml (accessed June 24, 2016).

Zhu, Y. X. 2015, March 11. Zhichi xiaowei xing minban xuexiao banxue (To support running small or micro private schools). *Zhongguo jiaoyu bao* (China Education News).

Addressing Sustainable International Branch Campus Development Through an Organizational Structure Lens: A Comparative Analysis of China, Qatar, and the United Arab Emirates

Jill Borgos

Abstract: The growth of international branch campuses (IBCs) in China, Qatar, and the United Arab Emirates (UAE) accounts for a significant portion of the overall growth of IBCs globally. Conversely the largest exporter of IBCs globally is the United States, with several U.S. IBCs located in each of these importing countries. With the intention of focusing on the largest importing countries and the largest exporting country in the development of IBCs, this article presents a comparative analysis of the development of U.S. IBCs in China, Qatar, and the UAE. The analysis serves to add to the discourse on how these organizations are designed and organized from a sustainability perspective to meet the educational demands and regulatory framework of the host country. The divergent strategies for IBC development employed in these three countries provide an ideal medium in which to comparatively explore the poorly understood complexities of IBC development in differing countries. The article draws on three key sources of information to highlight the comparatively different approaches to the organizational development of IBCs within each of the respective regions. To illuminate the differing organizational designs that have emerged in the three counties, this article situates the development of IBCs in a historical context, applies an organizational theory framework, and draws from primary qualitative data collected by the author. The author highlights that the different strategies in the organizational design of IBC business models in each of the three countries evolved due to specific economic strategies unique to the respective country and that the differing strategies are in part necessary for sustainability within the respective host country.

The types of business models emerging to support cross-border international higher education arrangements are numerous. The establishment of an international branch campuses (IBC) is one type of educational business model that has emerged to meet the demand for higher education globally. IBCs are a particularly attractive educational business model because they can potentially meet the demand for higher education without the time, expense, and labor-intensive investment required to build a higher education system from the ground up (Lane and Kinser 2011). Partly for this reason, IBC development is a growing phenomenon in transnational education, serving to augment a host country's higher education system in meeting and creating demand for higher education in locations with developing and transitional economies.

In a similar vein to the way corporate business ventures have grown in the global marketplace over the last several decades, the literature purports that IBCs are established based on a number of conditions specific to the country or region in which they are established. These conditions often include but are not limited to the availability of resources, cultural considerations, political instability, and the regulatory environment unique to the host country, the home country, and the program being delivered (Altbach 2011). Given these conditions, developing an IBC in a host country, similar to other global business ventures, is often complex and fraught with many unforeseen challenges (Altbach 2011). These challenges and complexities are not necessarily insurmountable barriers to the successful and sustainable development of IBCs globally, however further analysis of the ways in which IBCs are designed to ensure productive educational outcomes is necessary for future sustainable IBC development specific to a country or region. All successful IBC ventures will depend on the ability to adapt to the challenges, complexities, and educational needs unique to each country or region where an IBC is established. Due to the accelerated growth rate of IBCs over the last couple of decades, coupled with the differing innovative business arrangements delivering cross-border education in the form of an IBC, Lane and Kinser (2011) noted that the arrangements between the host country and the foreign institutions are often poorly understood.

The objective of this article is to better understand how IBC business model arrangements are designed, with the primary assumption that IBCs are designed with the intention of being healthy sustainable organizations. The article will specifically examine IBCs established by the United States in China, Qatar, and the United Arab Emirates (UAE). The author examines the development of IBCs in these countries by placing the development of IBCs in a historical context, viewing the design of the IBCs through an organizational behavior lens, and highlighting qualitative data collected by the author on IBC leadership and governance structures. An examination of IBCs in this way provides a unique perspective and contribution on how IBCs are arranged and designed with the purpose of providing a sustainable mode of delivery of cross-border higher education.

Illuminating the factors influencing the design of IBC business models requires an assessment of the overall economic strategies, the educational climate, and the potential growth in each of the respective counties. The unfolding of these layers reveals both similar economic strategies in the development of IBCs and differences in approaches to the design and organization of IBC business models. There is evidence of significant government involvement through strategic economic initiatives to educate a more globally competitive workforce in each of these countries. However, China with its expansive geography and the world's largest population at 1.4 billion began collaborative partnerships with foreign universities using a comparably different organizational arrangement of IBC models than the comparatively smaller countries Qatar and the UAE. The recent growth of IBCs within China is in part due to policy changes in China and it is also in part due to the inclusion of China's IBC partnership model as an accepted definition of what constitutes an IBC by organizations indexing IBCs, such as the Observatory of Borderless Higher Education (OBHE).

GROWTH OF IBCS

Defining an IBC

The definition of an IBC has evolved over time to include new and different arrangements of IBC development and in some cases what constitutes an IBC by definition is not universally agreed upon. The variation in IBC models emerging around the world makes the definition of an IBC a moving target (Becker 2009; Kinser 2010; Altbach 2011; Lawton and Katsomitros 2012). Lawton and Katsomitros (2012) noted that constant innovations in the way universities position themselves and variations in host country regulatory frameworks make settling on a definition challenging. Knight (2008) broadly defined cross-border higher education as any situation where a teacher, student, program, course materials, or institution cross national jurisdictional borders. IBCs as a form of cross-border higher education are most frequently and commonly defined as a higher education institution located in a different geopolitical region than the one in which the home campus originates or operates (Kinser 2010; Lawton and Katsomitros 2012). The OBHE further qualifies the definition of an IBC as having three key features. The IBC must maintain a physical presence in the host country, it must award at least one degree in the host country, and the degree program must be accredited in the country of the originating institution (Lawton and Katsomitros, IBC DATA and Developments [2012], p.7). The definition expanded from its original conception in 2009 by OBHE to currently include dual degree arrangements and the inclusion of institutions that offer part of a degree program at a branch campus as opposed to the entire degree (Lawton and Katsomitros 2012). This expanded definition is significant in that this definition proposed by OBHE enabled cross-border partnerships developing in China to be included and recognized as another type of IBC model (Lawton and Katsomitros 2012).

According to the Cross-Border Education Research Team (2015), one of a few organizations tracking data on IBCs, there are currently 229 IBCs in operation worldwide. Early developments of IBCs can be traced back to as early as 1933 when Florida State University began offering programs in Panama, and later in 1950 when Johns Hopkins University offered a program in Italy (Becker 2009; Lane 2011). During the 1980s a significant surge in IBC development occurred (Chambers and Cummings 1990; Lane 2011). During this time period several countries experienced rapid growth in their economies and in particular, developing economies were shifting their strategic focus to finding ways to align their education system with the workforce development needs of their country.

Few IBCs established during the 1980s still exist today[1] but a second wave of IBC growth has been taking place during the last two decades (Knight 2008). Advances in technology, infrastructure, and transportation are a few of the factors enabling the physical movement of institutions across geopolitical borders at a rate not previously seen (Knight 2008). Between 2006 and 2011 the number of IBCs grew in number from 85 to close to 200, which represented a 144% increase during this time period (Verbik and Merkley 2006; Lawton and Katsomitros 2012). Countries exporting the largest number of IBCs during this recent growth period include Australia, the United Kingdom, and the United States. Additionally, during the time period between 2006 and 2011, the United States represented the exporting country with the highest rate of overall growth in terms of newly established IBCs (Lawton and Katsomitros 2012).

CHINESE-FOREIGN COOPERATION IN RUNNING SCHOOLS

TABLE 1
Operational United States Branch Campuses in China (2015)

University of Pittsburgh, USA	China	United States
Sun Yat-sen University-Carnegie Mellon University Joint Institute of Engineering at Sun Yat-sen University	China	United States
Duke Kunshan University	China	United States
Fort Hays State University (Beijing)	China	United States
Fort Hays State University (Liaoning)	China	United States
Sias International University (Henan)	China	United States
Hopkins-Nanjing Center for Chinese and American Studies	China	United States
Wenzhou-Kean University	China	United States
LNU-MSU College of International Business	China	United States
Faculty of International Media, Communication University of China	China	United States
New York University Shanghai	China	United States
Sichuan University-Pittsburgh Institute	China	United States
Shanghai Jiao Tong University SJTU-UM Joint Institute	China	United States
NYIT-Nanjing	China	United States

Source: Cross-Border Education Research Team (2015).

TABLE 2
Operational United States Branch Campuses in Qatar (2015)

Carnegie Mellon University Qatar	Qatar	United States
Weill Cornell Medical College in Qatar	Qatar	United States
Georgetown University School of Foreign Service in Qatar	Qatar	United States
HCC in Qatar	Qatar	United States
Northwestern University in Qatar	Qatar	United States
Texas A&M University at Qatar	Qatar	United States
VCU Qatar	Qatar	United States

Source: Cross-Border Education Research Team (2015).

Of the 229 IBCs documented by the Cross-Border Education Research Team (2015), 27 are located in Mainland China and 43 are located in the Middle East region. For the purposes of this comparative analysis, the Middle East region includes the UAE and Qatar. The United States is responsible for 14, or a little more than half, of the IBCs currently in operation in China (Table 1).

In Qatar and the UAE, the United States is responsible for 13 of the 43 IBCs located in this region. Seven IBCs are located in Qatar (Table 2) and 6 IBCs are located in the UAE (Table 3).

TABLE 3
Operational United States Branch Campuses in the UAE (2015)

New York Film Academy Abu Dhabi	United Arab Emirates, Abu Dhabi	United States
NYIT-Abu Dhabi	United Arab Emirates, Abu Dhabi	United States
New York University Abu Dhabi	United Arab Emirates, Abu Dhabi	United States
Hult International Business School-Dubai Campus	United Arab Emirates, Dubai	United States
Michigan State University Dubai	United Arab Emirates, Dubai	United States
RIT Dubai	United Arab Emirates, Dubai	United States

Source: Cross-Border Education Research Team (2015).

HISTORICAL DEVELOPMENT OF IBCS BY COUNTRY

Development of IBCs in China

Three significant events in China have contributed to driving higher education policy development and subsequently the growth of IBCs. Contributing factors in the growth of IBCs in China include the globalization of the world economy, the opening up of China, and China's large student population (Xu and Kan 2013). In many ways the expanding educational policies that have emerged in the most populated country in the world mirror early developments in globalization and the global growth in goods and services post World War II (WWII).

WWII marked the beginning of an early period of globalization and a new era in the global trade of goods and services. However, the new era began with limited involvement of China in the global trade of goods and services, which was in sharp contrast to Europe's heavy involvement. By 1980, the Europe led the way in the global market with the highest share of both world exports (40.9%) and global gross domestic product (GDP); 27.8%) (United Nations Conference on Trade and Development 2012). In contrast, China's share of world exports was approximately 1% and its share of the global GDP was 2.4% (United Nations Conference on Trade and Development 2012). However, running parallel to this same period and the growing global market was the development of key strategic education policies in China. These key educational strategies would lead to collaborative Chinese foreign partnerships two decades later and contribute to China being ranked fifth in the world in its number of foreign enrollments by 2007 (Hvistendahl 2008).

Under the leadership of Deng Xiaoping, China, a historically closed society, made a strategic decision in 1978 to significantly increase the number of Chinese students studying abroad (Xu and Kan 2013). This policy decision was one of many policy and regulatory changes impacting the educational environment in China. The 1980s education reform is documented as one of the pioneering strategies in China's opening up with the intent that the educational reform strategies were designed with the "strategic foresight of the Chinese nation to develop education and build confidence in China's education system" (Ministry of Education of the People's Republic of China 2010a).

By 1996, or approximately 15 years after the opening up of China, China had doubled its share of world exports to 2.6%. Five years later China joined the World Trade Organization (WTO) and by 2010 it was "on the way to becoming the top merchandise and services exporter" (United Nations Conference on Trade and Development 2012). China's membership in the WTO in 2001 marked an increase in global market trading. Concurrently, China joining the WTO also accelerated the development of higher education policy in China (Xu and Kan 2013). Supporting rhetoric in China's New National Education Plan stating that China "plans to become a country with rich human resources" suggests that changes to national strategy in the advancement of educational opportunities were formulated in response to the thriving global economy driven by a knowledge based society (Ministry of Education of the People's Republic of China 2010a). And in China, with A Blueprint for Educational Modernization, statements such as "A strong nation requires quality education, and quality education is a prerequisite for national development" also pinpoint the connection and strategic efforts linking expanding educational opportunities with the overall development of a nation (Ministry of Education of the People's Republic of China 2010b).

The policies impacting China's higher education have changed significantly since the reform and opening up in 1978, but the changes in China's education system have predominately evolved at a higher rate since China joined the WTO in 2001 (Xu and Kan 2013) and the changes parallel economic development strategies. In 2001, as part of China's membership in the WTO, China committed to more robust trade agreements in educational services. This commitment "opened the educational market to foreign providers in broad fields" (Xu and Kan 2013, 205). China's now more open educational market enabled foreign providers to partner in joint ventures such as IBCs. In 2003, documents were published supporting growth with foreign partners. In *Regulations of the People's Republic of China on Chinese-Foreign Cooperation in Running Schools*, China's Ministry of Education encourages cooperation with foreign education institutions. China's Ministry of Education outlined several general provisions with articles stating that "Chinese–foreign cooperation needed to meet the needs of Chinese citizens, be of high quality, not compromise China's sovereignty, and that the State Council is responsible for the macro control of Chinese-foreign cooperative activities" (Ministry of Education of the People's Republic of China 2003). General provisions in the aforementioned policy document highlight China's attempt to maintain oversight of the establishment and organizational structures of IBCs established in China through foreign cooperative relationships.

The University of Nottingham Ningbo China (UNNC) IBC represents one of the earliest forms of the accelerated higher education activities involving Chinese –foreign cooperative relations. While construction was underway for the new UNNC campus in 2004, the first cohort of students was enrolled at the campus (Feng 2013). The Chinese partnership with an elite British university highlights some of the unique aspects of the policies governing the Chinese-foreign partnerships. A particularly unique aspect of the policies governing the establishment of IBCs in China requires that the President of any joint international campus venture within China must be a Chinese citizen (Feng 2013). In this particular case, the newly appointed Chancellor of the University of Nottingham home campus in 2000 happened to be a Chinese citizen. Yang Fujia, the sixth Chancellor of the University of Nottingham, led the way in the collaboration with China and as a Chinese citizen served the role as President of UNNC which Feng (2013) noted, "made him the best person to meet Chinese regulation and to ensure the British interest" (477).

As joint ventures in China continued to expand in the decade following the UNNC collaboration, different arrangements have evolved between China and foreign higher education partners. In a similar vein as the UNNC model, involvement of the Chinese government, and/or its citizens per China's education policies, is the same with partnerships and management of the joint ventures between U.S. universities and China. Recent arrangements between elite U.S. universities and China include the establishment of the Duke-Kunshan University campus in partnership with Wuhan University, and New York University's partnership with East China Normal University in Shanghai (Feng 2013). Similarly, organizational structures of U.S. IBCs in China highlight the close involvement of China's government in the partnership and management of IBCs.

Development of IBCs in Qatar

Qatar, a peninsula nation located in the Arab Gulf region, is home to approximately 2.1 million people (World Bank Data 2014) and by comparison to China it is a much smaller country with a singular but rich natural resource, petroleum products. Even though declining oil reserves compromised the nation's revenues during the 1980s and early 1990s, Qatar's leadership during this time was able to diversify the economy to an extent which enabled the creation of additional revenues streams outside of its natural gas production (Gonzalez et al. 2008). The nation demonstrated a large growth in per capita GDP of an average of 28,000 USD in 2002 up from 14,000 USD in the 1990s (Gonzalez et al. 2008). The tremendous wealth Qatar has been able to achieve over the last 60 years has enabled Qatar to strategically plan for a future when petroleum products will not generate the revenue needed to support the country. To compete in an era defined by a global economy and a knowledge society, Sheikh Hamad Bin Khalifa recognized that Qatar's government needed to invest in educating its population to increase the diversity of human capital and to build a knowledge society within Qatar (Krieger 2008). By doing so, the nation of Qatar could position itself to compete in markets outside of the oil and natural gas industry and to better ensure economic sustainability in the face of dwindling oil and natural gas.

The Qatar Foundation, a nonprofit organization supported by the Qatar government and under the leadership of Sheikh Hamad Bin Khalifa's wife Sheika Mozah Bint Nasser Al Missned, was established to address the educational, scientific research, and community development needs of Qatar's future (Krieger 2008). In recognizing the dearth of higher education institutions in Qatar, the Qatar Foundation systematically created what is known as Education City in Doha. Education City is considered a hub of higher education made up of six American university branch campuses offering a diverse range of educational opportunities for both Qataris and other non-nationals. The Qatar Foundation shoulders all the cost for the operations of these branch campuses in Education City, and also contributes an undisclosed amount in fees to the universities themselves (Krieger 2008). Carnegie Mellon University, Weill Cornell Medical College, Northwestern University, Texas A&M University, Virginia Commonwealth University, and Georgetown University of Foreign Service are the few select U.S. universities who were invited and accepted the opportunity to establish campuses and provide their degree-awarding programs from a physical location in Qatar. Although the extent of the Qatar Foundation's financial commitment to the branch campuses is atypical of IBCs globally, this particular arrangement does represent one aspect of the type of partnerships developing between foreign universities and the host countries. As is the case in China, the development of IBCs in Qatar is in response to a country's national strategy to build educational capacity within the country without building an educational system from the ground up.

Development of IBCs in the UAE

In the UAE, IBC development occurred as one part of a larger economic development plan, similar to that which occurred in China and Qatar. Dubai, one of the seven Emirates comprising the UAE, emerged as the fastest growing Emirate within the UAE in terms of the overall number of IBCs. Parallel to the historical development of Qatar, Dubai in the 19th century was a tribal community with a strategic seaport known for its fishing, pearling, and sea trade. The discovery of oil in Dubai in 1966, however, triggered an influx of foreign workers and spurred a trade economy beyond that tied to the strategic waterways (Gulf News 2010; BBC News 2015). Sheik Rashid, ruler of Dubai, used the newfound oil wealth to develop schools, hospitals, roads and the telecommunication network to support advancement of the economy and society (Government of Dubai 2015). While the discovery of oil brought great prosperity to the region and diversified the workforce with expatriates, by the 1980s and early 1990s, Dubai, with a smaller proportion of oil reserves than other Emirates in UAE, strategically began to plan for diversifying its economy beyond oil (BBC News 2015). With its reserves expected to be exhausted within 20 years, Dubai moved forward with a vision to become a tourism destination (Gulf News 2010; Government of Dubai 2015).

Dubai had a young and limited higher education system with its first higher education institution, United Arab Emirates University opening its doors in 1976 (Lane 2010b). Since the late 1970s Dubai's higher education environment has changed significantly in response to the fast growing global economy and the need for a diversified workforce. Similar to the historical development of IBCs in China and Qatar, the government of Dubai recognized the need to provide greater access to higher education and to do so with an alacrity that would allow Dubai to keep pace with the global economy. Again, such as was the case in China and Qatar, the import of foreign universities provided an efficient means to establish university structures and curriculum without the years of growth needed to build a new higher education institution from a nascent state. A catalyst to the rapid growth of foreign institutions in Dubai stemmed from the establishment of tax-free zones in the region. The tax-free zones, conceptualized long before the idea of IBCs, were established in Dubai under the leadership of Sheikh Rashid to further accelerate commercial activity around Dubai's port after the discovery of the oil fields (Government of Dubai 2015). These tax-free zones provided an enticing environment for foreign institutions to establish IBCs with exemption from federal regulation (Lane 2010b). Lane (2010b) notes, that the free zones in Dubai "have been one of the most important factors in the growth of foreign education providers in Dubai" (4).

ORGANIZATIONAL PERSPECTIVE ON IBC DEVELOPMENT

IBC Business Model

The complex organizational dynamics of opening a branch campus in a host country introduces challenges to the delivery of cross-border education that need to be addressed to provide a sustainable delivery model of higher education. While the opportunities for expanding the capacity for higher education is growing through the establishment of IBCs, there are a multitude of associated risks. Kinser (2010) noted that there are inevitably links among the IBC, the home campus, and the host country. For example, the links can occur through partnerships with for-profit companies, government entities, or private foundations depending on the regulatory environment unique to the host country (Kinser 2010). The sustainability of a branch campus will depend on the ability of both the home institution and the host country to negotiate conditions in order for IBCs as organizations to flourish. Regardless of whether an IBC is established as a solo investment or through a partnership, thoughtful consideration of the organizational structure is essential to maximize sustainability and reduce financial risk and undesirable closure.

Within the landscape of the various IBC models, there are three more commonly found organizational structures. These organizational models are categorized based on the financial model in which the IBCs were established. The three predominate categories of IBCs models include those that are wholly owned, those that are joint ventures, and those that are strategic alliances (Verbik and Merkley 2006; Lane 2011). The wholly owned model is considered the most risky and involves the home campus being responsible for both the financial investment and the navigation of the host country's idiosyncratic legal and regulatory environment (Verbik and Merkley 2006; Lane 2010a). In contrast to the wholly owned model with solo aspirations, the joint venture model involves the establishment of an IBC as a negotiated entity between two or more entities with a vested interest in the success of the IBC (Garrett 2002). The joint venture model often includes some variation in the sharing of the financial risks and rewards, collaboration on curriculum, and the sharing of physical space (Verbik and Merkley 2006). Strategic alliances as described by Lane (2010a) are a category of IBCs operating somewhere between a wholly owned branch campus and a joint venture. Verbik and Merkley (2006) further emphasize that a key component of a strategic alliance is that the funding for the IBC is either generated by the host country or from some other private company or organization in the home or host country. In most cases the IBC is operating in the host country via an invitation with the initial funding source coming from regional or central authorities in the host country (Verbik and Merkley 2006). Similar to IBCs established through the efforts of joint ventures, strategic alliances often involve some sharing of resources such as the host country providing the physical space for the IBC. Unlike joint ventures, IBCs established as a strategic alliance are often organized in a manner that allows the home campus to maintain responsibility for the management of the physical space, the curriculum, and the awarding of degrees (Verbik and Merkley 2006). In Qatar and the UAE strategic alliances are more common (Lane 2010a). Joint venture arrangements are more commonly found in countries where the host country regulatory policies mandate that a foreign institution partner with a host country entity, such as the case with IBCs established in China (Kinser 2010; Lawton and Katsomitros 2012).

Location, Location, Location

The different patterns emerging in the organizational structures of IBCs represent a departure from a commonly held perspective found in institutional theory, which is that organizations within a particular field, such as education, adopt similar structures leading them to become more isomorphic over time regardless of location (DiMaggie and Powell 1983). Institutional theory posits that institutions will adopt similar structures to manage resources, consumers, key suppliers, and regulatory agencies (DiMaggie and Powell 1983). The isomorphic patterns develop due to a particular field or industry seeking legitimacy and using similar services associated with key suppliers, resources, consumers, and regulatory agencies (DiMaggie and Powell 1983). Contrary to the premise of institutional theory the variation in emerging IBC business models suggests that IBCs as organizations are designed differently country to country with fewer isomorphic patterns evident, despite having a similar goal of delivering higher education. In the case of IBCs as organizational institutions, location does matter.

This holds true for IBCs originating from the same home country. Within a single home country, institution-to-institution, isomorphic patterns in the delivery of education are found, but when traveling across borders, variations in business models are found. This variation points to a process of adaptation and the differences are suggestive of the ways in which legitimacy, resources, suppliers, and consumers are acquired differently depending on the geopolitical location. This adaptive process is strategic for organizational sustainability when moving an organization across geopolitical borders. In this way, resource dependence theory better situates the organizational behavior found in the establishment of IBCs as institutions.

Resource dependence theory provides an alternative context in which to better understand how and why IBCs are emerging in a variety of different models. Resource dependence theory posits that, "organizations are inescapably bound up within the conditions of their environment" (Pfeffer and Salancik 2003, 1). Pfeffer and Salancik (2003) suggested that the characteristics of an organization are reflective of the environment in which they operate and that these characteristics or behaviors are evidence of strategy for survival unique to the specific environment in which the organization operates. How an organization manages its dependence on the environment in which it operates will in part determine the sustainability of the organization. Scott and Davis (2007) noted that resource dependence theory is useful in understanding the ways in which organizations use differing types of tactics and strategies to minimize uncertainty and manage their relations with others in their environment. In this way, resource dependence theory helps to illuminate how IBCs are designed differently country to country based on the conditions of their environment to manage issues related to legitimacy, key suppliers, resources, consumers, and regulatory agencies.

One of the key strategies used by organizations to manage their dependence and uncertainty is through the use of relationships or social networks. Early research by Granovetter (1974) found that people tend to prefer conducting business with people familiar to them or within their social networks and pointed out that this is especially true under conditions of uncertainty (Pfeffer and Salancik 2003). Familiar connections offer trust and security, which in turn can foster positive relationships in the face of an uncertain business environment (Peng and Luo 2000). In countries and regions with developing and transitional economies where IBCs are established, social connections have been found to be a key strategy for business exchanges and development (Acquaah 2007). Acquaah (2007, 1236) noted that "the strong collectivistic cultures in emerging economies such as Africa, the Middle East, and Asia " where IBCs are prevalent and growing are examples of and understanding of regions where social or familial connections can be found as a significant strategy for conducting business. In research conducted by the author on interconnections between IBC leadership and the host country, Borgos (2013) found similar evidence of social and familial connections in the governance and leadership structures of U.S. IBCs in a variety of countries and regions. These findings suggested that IBCs have adopted a key adaptive strategy in the use of relationships to manage uncertainty in a foreign environment. In the case of U.S. IBC development in China, Qatar, and the UAE, the diverse geopolitical environments in which IBCs operate changes how organizational structures such as governance and leadership are designed to meet the demands of the geopolitically and culturally different suppliers, resources, consumers, and regulatory agencies (Borgos 2013).

Governance and Leadership

In 2013 I collected data as part of a qualitative study on IBC governance and leadership structures to further understand the ways in which IBCs were connecting to the host country and to identify the types of organizational leadership and governance structures that were emerging at each of the IBCs. The study utilized qualitative social network analysis to identify relationships and patterns found among the individuals holding leadership positions at IBCs. Using ATLAS.ti concept mapping (ATLAS.ti Scientific Software Development GmbH, Berlin, Germany), patterns of interconnections were uncovered in terms of density of connections, themes, and common patterns (Scott 2010; Friese 2012). Data were collected through a comprehensive web based search of 48 U.S. IBCs in seven geographic areas examining IBC leadership and governance structures. The study explored the on-site administrative structures, board structures, and used qualitative social network analysis to identify relationships between the home and the host country through administrative and board structures.

A key finding of the study supports the premise of resource dependence theory in that IBCs as organizations have the ability to use strategies such as social networking or relationships to adapt and minimize uncertainty to support sustainable outcomes, especially in foreign environments. The study found six prevalent relationship patterns between the IBCs and the host country environment. The study specifically examined interconnections identified between IBC board members or the administrative staff on-site and the host country. The relationship themes found between an IBC and its respective host country included (1) an on-site IBC administrator at some point was previous employed by an organization based in the host country, (2) an on-site IBC administrator at some point was previous employed by a host country postsecondary institution, (3) an on-site IBC administrator attained an undergraduate or graduate degree in the host country, (4) an on-site administrator is native to or has familial relations in the host country or region, (5) the IBC as an organization is part of a partnership with a host country university or educational consulting company, and (6) in the case of IBCs with governance boards, IBC board members worked for industries in or governments of the host country directly related to the types of programs offered by the IBC (Borgos 2013).

The most commonly identified connections between IBC leadership and the host country included an administrator having been previously employed by an organization or postsecondary institution in the host country. This occurred with greater frequency in IBCs established in Qatar, however it is not unique to IBCs established in Qatar. In both Qatar and the UAE, a number of IBCs are established with board structures and in these cases the density of connections found between the IBC and the host country or region were high. The board members were almost always employed by industries operating in that country or region, or they were government officials in the host country. This relationship can provide knowledge of the local environment in terms of operating a business, acquiring resources, or sharing in a vested interest in the sustainability of the IBC. Last, a common connection found was between organization to organization through a business relationship between a host country educational partnership or educational consulting company and that of the IBC (See Table 1). IBCs in China are the most consistent example of this type of connection. Each of these relationships found in the study in some way can provide avenues to adopt practices compatible with the local environment and provide access to resources, suppliers, consumers (students), and knowledge of regulatory policies.

A second descriptive finding from the author's study highlights the organizational behavior of IBCs in terms of the variation in IBC leadership structures being utilized. As a result of the findings, an American International Branch Campus Leadership Typology was created that identifies six distinct categories of IBC leadership structure found at IBCs established by

U.S. higher education institutions (HEIs). The typology classified IBCs based on five patterns of leadership structure that emerged during the collection of data. The patterns included (1) the size of the administrative staff, (2) the presence or absence of a board structure, (3) the arrangement of a partnership with either the host country or an educational consulting group, (4) the interconnectedness between the administrative on-site leadership and the host country, and (5) the interconnects found between IBC board members and the host country.

Out of the six categories in the American International Branch Campus Leadership Typology, IBC leadership structures in Qatar and China are predominately found in two different and distinctive categories. In contrast, the leadership structures of IBCs in the UAE can be found in several different categories within the typology. These findings further challenge the institutional theory premise that isomorphic patterns emerge when a HEI physically moves and operates in a geopolitical environment different than that of the home campus. Rather we variation in the structure of IBCs allowing them to adapt to the environment in which the institution operates.

Despite the different types leadership and governance structures identified in the study (Borgos 2013) that are suggestive of organizations adapting differently to the foreign environment in which they operate, parallels can be found in the development of IBCs in China, Qatar, and the UAE. In each country the development of IBCs is linked to an overall national strategy for higher education in relationship to the historic growth of the global economy. The combination of the differences in leadership structures region to region, coupled with the national strategy for higher education in each region, leads to reflection in two different ways. In one way it is interesting to reflect on how IBCs, despite originating from the home country where educational organizations for the most part resemble each other (DiMaggie and Powell 1983), display differing organizational structures when the campus opens a branch across borders. In a second way it is interesting to reflect on why these differing IBCs models exist country to country with supportive mechanism in the form of relationships and connections between the IBC and the host country. Based on the patterns of leadership structures found in the typology, IBCs established by U.S. HEIs in China, Qatar, and the UAE emerged in different categories within the typology despite originating from the same home country.

DIFFERENCES IN ORGANIZATIONAL STRUCTURES OF U.S. IBCS IN CHINA, QATAR, AND THE UNITED ARAB EMIRATES

China's Sino-International Relations

The organizational design of U.S. IBCs in China is predominately driven by China's regulatory policy requiring foreign institutions to partner with a Chinese university. For this reason all IBCs established by U.S. HEIs in China are classified in Borgos' (2013) typology as Category IV. Category IV IBCs were found to have a small administrative staff (less than Five members), no presence of a governing board structure,[2] and they were established as a partnership arrangement or created through the support of an educational consulting group. The partnership or educational consulting arrangement was a unique and distinctive factor for IBCs placed in this category. IBCs established in other countries fall into this category as well, such as City

University of Seattle in Switzerland or Carnegie Mellon University in Australia. However, it is not the case that IBCs established by the same home campus would fall into the same Category if they are established in different countries. Carnegie Mellon University in Australia is classified as a Category IV in the typology (Borgos 2013) but Carnegie Mellon University in Qatar is classified in a different category. This suggests that regardless of the originating home campus, the region in which the IBC is established whether it is China, Qatar, or Australia, for example, is a determining factor in the way in which IBC structures are designed.

Two examples of Sino-international relations between U.S. HEIs and China include New York Institute of Technology's (NYIT) collaboration with Nanjing University of Posts and Telecommunication and Johns Hopkins University's collaboration with Nanjing University. NYIT-Nanjing was the first American undergraduate IBC in China and is accredited by both China's Ministry of Education and the Commission on Higher Education of the Middle States Association of Colleges and Schools (NYIT-China 2015). The Hopkins-Nanjing Center represents the first joint academic program in China to offer a masters' degree fully accredited in China and the United States. In both examples there is a small administrative staff with codirectors who have connections to China and the existence of shared facilities such as residence halls and conference sites. These types of IBC arrangements are highly prevalent in China.

Qatar's Strategic Alliances

In comparison to U.S. IBCs in China and the UAE, IBCs in Qatar are more similar in organizational structures to institutions on the home campus. The development of Education City by the Qatar Foundation features IBC Joint advisory boards as a governance structure. The branch campuses in Qatar have boards with specific responsibilities that are narrower than conventional home campus boards. Joint advisory boards are not equivalent to the home campus governing board, but are designed to provide advice regarding management and operation of the branch as well as being responsible for ongoing review and evaluation of the success of the program (The Qatar Foundation 2015). Board membership at the U.S. IBCs in Qatar consists of equal representation of members representing the home campus and the host country. The membership of the joint advisory boards reveals a pattern of significant connectedness between the home institution and the host country. Members of the joint advisory boards are connected to government and industries within the region. In each of the IBCs the on-site administrative staff structure resembles a scaled down version of the home campus (Borgos 2013). The administrative on-site staff is structured with various combinations of deans, and associate deans, as well as communication, finance, academic affairs, and human resource personnel. In many instances these administrative staff were connected in some way to the host country.

In the American International Branch Campus Leadership Typology (Borgos 2013) the IBCs in Qatar within the same category. The category included IBCs that operate with relatively large on-site administrative staffs as compared to other IBC arrangements. The category also included IBCs with relatively large board structures and through these board structures a significant number of connections between the board members and the host country were identified either through industry, government, or other education entities.

United Arab Emirates' Free Zones

The free zones in the UAE, in particular free zones in Dubai, dictated the geographic organization of the IBCs established in this region. The four free zones in Dubai host a significant number of IBCs in this region. The four free zones include Dubai International Academic City/Dubai Knowledge Village, Dubai International Financial City, Dubai Health Care City, and Dubai Silicon Oasis (Cross-Border Education Research Team 2015). DIAC/DKV is the only free zone dedicated to education and is home to over 20 international universities and 4,000 students (Lane 2010b; Cross-Border Education Research Team 2015) Abu Dhabi's capital city is host to a few IBCs and functions as a hub, although not in the aggressive fashion as is the case in Dubai. The free zones essentially enable Dubai to recruit foreign institutions, at least initially, with a minimalist regulatory burden. This approach was meant to encourage rapid growth in program and curriculum offerings in a region with limited educational opportunities. The IBCs, as Lane (2010b) reported, enabled the UAE to absorb demand for higher education, provided something different than the existing institutions, signaled modernity, and created new demand from students who wanted the education provided by the IBCs. The early regulatory framework and free zone structure reflects directly in the variety of administrative and leadership structures identified in the Typology of American International Branch Campus Leadership (Borgos 2013). The U.S. IBCs in the UAE have differences in the size of their administrative staff and may or may not have a representative board. The somewhat flexible regulatory environment enabled a diverse collection of organizational structures in that they did not need to conform to a set policy outlining how the IBCs were to be established and managed. New York University-Abu Dhabi and Duke University-Dubai are examples of U.S. IBCs in the UAE that are classified in different categories within the typology. New York University operates in Abu Dhabi with a large on-site administrative staff, but there is no evidence of a board structure. In contrast Duke University operating a campus in Dubai was found to have both a relatively small on-site administrative staff and a board structure. Similar to the board member connections to the host country in Qatar through the joint advisory board structure, the board members associated with Duke's IBC in Dubai were found to have a number of connections to the industries within the region.

CONCLUSION

IBC Sustainability

The way in which IBCs are structured is unique in each of the three countries discussed in this article. How best to establish IBCs as sustainable organizations moving across borders is still debatable. However, in each of these three countries IBCs have been established in part as a result of the host country's educational policies (China), economic development policies (UAE's Free Zones), or alliances by invitation with considerable financial investments from the host country (Qatar). The variation in business models and the relative infancy of IBC development makes it difficult to truly assess the complexities and issues that may compromise the sustainability of IBCs, but several notable concerns have been raised in key areas (Altbach 2010; Altbach 2011). Regardless of the structure or business model established, similar concerns embrace IBCs in any location. Enrollment numbers, sources of revenue, quality of curriculum, availability of faculty, and changing local conditions have been frequently cited as key areas potentially impacting the degree to which an IBC can maintain a sustainable presence in a host country. In particular, low enrollment of students at many IBCs is a significant concern. Altbach (2011) notes that for institutions such as Northwestern University (Qatar) and New York University (Abu Dhabi, Shanghai), the availability of students meeting the qualification standards for these selective institutions is debatable and further imparts justification to the debate on the long term sustainability of IBCs.

Any organization moving across geopolitical borders, regardless as to whether it is a multinational company or an educational entity, will face unique challenges in each environment in which it operates. However, identifying and managing these obstacles becomes paramount for organizations to survive and fulfill the intended purpose of their endeavor (Knight 2006; Altbach 2010, 2011; Hughes 2011; Kinser 2011; Lane 2011). The success of an organization in part will depend on its ability to make connections within the host country and to manage its dependency on the foreign external environment in which it operates (Pfeffer and Salancik 2003). When educational entities move across borders, the resources, consumers, key suppliers, and regulatory agencies differ from country to country and it is unlikely that similar organizational and structural patterns of IBCs will look the same country to country despite originating from the same home country (Borgos 2013). The variation in IBC models demonstrates in some ways the adaptation needed to move an educational entity or any organization across geopolitical borders. In the case of the three countries examined in the paper, China, Qatar, and the UAE the IBCs established display organizational structures consistent with adaptation to the environment in which they are operating.

The different and unique connections and structural arrangements illuminate adaptation of IBCs as organizations operating globally. In the case of regions with the largest growth in the number of IBCs, (China, Qatar, and the UAE), differences are found in IBC models country to country. The differences can be linked to historical developments respective of national strategies to increase educational capacities. By increasing educational capacity they are able to diversify educational offerings to support a workforce for current and future economic development and to participate in the rapidly changing global market. The sustainability of IBCs remains open to debate, however differing organizational models of IBCs country to country suggests adaptation to the local environment as an essential step for any organization moving their operations across geopolitical borders. The ability of IBCs to build associations and connections enabling a flow of information and knowledge about the local environment will be paramount to their long-term sustainability.

NOTES

1. Most of the 1980s growth was centered in Japan, and most of those IBCs never survived the decade (Altbach, 2011).

2. While governing boards at IBCs in China were not found as part of the organizational structure in the IBCs examined, some current IBCs in China now seem to have a governing or executive board (Borgos 2013). For example, Duke-Kunshan University is organized with both a board of trustees and an advisory board. By virtue of the partnership arrangement between Duke University and Wuhan University, the IBC would still be classified in Category IV of the typology.

REFERENCES

Acquaah, M. 2007. Managerial social capital, strategic orientation, and organizational performance in an emerging economy. *Strategic Management Journal* 28:1235–55. doi:10.1002/smj.632

Altbach, P. G. 2010. Why branch campuses may be unsustainable. *International Higher Education* 58:2–3.

Altbach, P. G. 2011. Is there a future for branch campuses? *International Higher Education* 65 (Fall):7–10.

BBC News. 2015, February 24. United Arab Emirates profile-overview. *BBC News*. http://www.bbc.com/news/world-middle-east-14703998

Becker, R. F. J. 2009. *International branch campuses: Markets and strategies*. London: Observatory on Borderless Higher Education.

Borgos, C. J. 2013. An Examination of Interconnectedness between U.S. international branch campuses and their host countries. PhD Diss., Univerity at Albany, State Univeristy of New York.

Chambers, G. S., and K. W. Cummings. 1990. *Profiting from education. Japan-United States international educational ventures in the 1980s. IIE research report number twenty*. New York: Institute of International Education.

Cross-Border Education Research Team. 2015. C-BERT branch campus listings. [Data originally collected by Kevin Kinser and Jason E. Lane].

DiMaggie, P. J., and W. Powell. 1983. The iron cage revisited: Institutional isomorphism and collective rationality in organizational fields. *American Sociological Review* 48:147–60. doi:10.2307/2095101

Feng, Y. 2013. University of Nottingham Ningbo China and Xi'an Jiaotong-Liverpool University: Globalization of higher education in China. *Higher Education* 65:471–85. doi:10.1007/s10734-012-9558-8

Friese, S. 2012. *Qualitative data analysis with* ATLAS.ti. Los Angeles: Sage.

Garrett, R. 2002. *International branch campuses: Scale and significance*. London: Observatory on Borderless Higher Education.

Gonzalez, G. C., L. A. Karoly, L. Constant, H. Salem, and C. A. Goldman. 2008. *Facing human capital challenges of the 21 Century: Education and labor market initiatives in Lebanon, Oman, Qatar, and the United Arab Emirates*. Doha: Rand Corporation-Qatar Policy Institute.

Government of Dubai. 2015. Dubai history. http://www.dubai.ae/en/aboutdubai/Pages/DubaiHistory.aspx (accessed September 10, 2015).

Gulf News. 2010, February 4. Oil in Dubai: History & timeline, A look at Dubai's history and key moments in oil production and export. http://gulfnews.com/business/oil-in-dubai-history-timeline-1.578333

Granovetter, M. S. 1974. *Getting a job*. Cambridge, MA: Harvard University Press.

Hughes, R. 2011. Strategies for managing and leading an academic staff in multiple countries. In *Multinational Colleges and Universities: Leading, Governing, and Managing International Branch Campuses*, ed. J. E. Lane and K. Kinser 19–28. San Francisco: Wiley.

Hvistendahl, M. 2008. China moves up as fifth importer of students. *Chronicle of Higher Education* 55 (4):A1.

Kinser, K. 2010. The private nature of cross-border higher education. In *The global growth of private higher education*, ed. ASHE Higher Education Report, 107–18. Hoboken: Jossey-Bass.

Kinser, K. 2011. Multinational quality assurance. In *Multinational Colleges and Universities: Leading, Governing, and Managing International Branch Campuses*, ed. J. E. Lane and K. Kinser 53–64. San Francisco: Wiley Periodicals, Inc.

Knight, J. 2006. *Higher education crossing borders: A guide to the implications of the general agreement on trade in services (gats) for cross-border education*. Paris: Commonwealth of Learning, UNESCO.

Knight, J. 2008. The role of cross-border education in the debate on education as a public good and private commodity. *Journal of Asian Public Policy* 1:174–87. doi:10.1080/17516230802094478

Krieger, Z. 2008. Academic building boom transforms the Persian Gulf. *Education Digest*, no. 74.

Lane, J. E. 2010a. Joint ventures in cross-border higher education: International branch campuses in Malaysia. In *Cross-border partnerships in higher education: Strategies and issues*, ed. D. W. Chapman and R. Sakamoto. London: Routledge.

Lane, J. E. 2010b. International Branch Campuses, Free Zones, and Quality Assurance: Policy Issues for Dubai and the UAE. Dubai School of Government Policy Brief No. 20:1–8.

Lane, J. E. 2011. Global expansion of international branch campuses: Managerial and leadership challenges. In *Multinational colleges and universities: Leading, governing, and managing international branch campuses*, ed. J. Lane and K. Kinser. San Francisco: Jossey-Bass.

Lane, J. E., and K. Kinser. 2011. Reconsidering privatization in cross-border engagements: The sometimes public nature of private activity. *Higher Education Policy* 24:255–73. doi:10.1057/hep.2011.2

Lawton, W., and A. Katsomitros. 2012. International branch campuses: Data and developments. *The Observatory on Borderless Higher Education.*

Ministry of Education of the People's Republic of China. 2003. Regulation of the people's republic of China on Chinese-Foreign cooperation in running schools. http://www.moe.edu.cn/publicfiles/business/htmlfiles/moe/moe_861/200506/8646.html (accessed September 15, 2015).

Ministry of Education of the People's Republic of China. 2010a. China's new national education plan aims to build a country with rich human resources. http://www.moe.edu.cn/publicfiles/business/htmlfiles/moe/s3501/201010/109031.html (accessed September 15, 2015).

Ministry of Education of the People's Republic of China. 2010b. A blueprint for educational modernization. http://www.moe.edu.cn/publicfiles/business/htmlfiles/moe/s3501/201010/109029.html (accessed September 15, 2015).

NYIT-China. 2015. New York Institute of Technology-Nanjing. http://www.nyit.edu/china/about/ (accessed October 10, 2015).

Peng, M. W., and Y. Luo. 2000. Managerial ties and firm performance in a transition economy: The nature of a micro-macro link. *Academy of Management Journal* 43:486–501.

Pfeffer, J., and G. R. Salancik. 2003. *The external control of organizations: A resource dependency perspective.* Stanford, CA: Stanford University Press.

Scott, J. 2010. *Social network analysis a handbook.* Los Angeles: Sage.

Scott, R., and G. Davis. 2007. The dyadic environment of the organization. In *Organizations and Organizing: Rational, Natural, and Open System Perspective*, ed. R. Scott and G. Davis. Englewood Cliffs, NJ: Pearson.

The Qatar Foundation. 2015. Joint advisory boards. http://www.qf.org.qa (accessed August 1, 2015).

United Nations Conference on Trade and Development. 2012. Development and globalization: Facts & figures 2012. http://dgff.unctad.org/chapter1/1.1.html

Verbik, L., and C. Merkley. 2006. The International Branch Campus - Models and Trends. *The Observatory on Borderless Higher Education.*

World Bank. 2014. World Bank data: Qatar. http://data.worldbank.org/country/qatar

Xu, X., and Y. Kan. 2013. Cross-border higher education in China in the globalized world: The perspective of the World Trade Organization's general agreement on trade services. *Journal of Educational Policy* 10 (2):199–230.

Hong Kong's Cross-System University Partnerships

Gerard A. Postiglione, Qin Yunyun, and Alice Y.C. Te

Abstract: The authors examine the special case of Hong Kong higher education's institutional partnerships in the Chinese mainland. After noting the rise of cross-system university partnership in Asia, it provides a neoinstitutional perspective on the differences between the two China higher education systems. Finally, a case study of the experience of the longest-running Hong Kong campus partnership on the Chinese mainland is discussed and analyzed. Results show that while adaptations are required to sustain the partnership, the degree of autonomy has grown over time.

Universities are organizational actors. The same holds true for the growing number of partnership universities that span different systems. Universities involved in partnerships have different roles and resource constraints. University models across the world begin to seem more common, but historical roots create path dependencies. Here we examine selected aspects of academic partnerships of China's two university systems: Hong Kong and the Chinese mainland. We situate the analysis within the larger context of eastern Asia's expanding cross-border university partnerships. By providing data on the rising number of partnerships between universities in China's two systems, we identify characteristics of the partnership programs. We argue that Hong Kong programs on the Chinese mainland maintain key aspects of its model, but operate in a bubble with little effect on wider system of higher education. The most successful case reveals a hybrid model that retains the character of universities in Hong Kong, along with adaptations to the campus ethos on the Chinese mainland.

The 21st century will probably be remembered as ushering in a globalization of higher education, with a model driven by the rapid increase in cross system campuses, degree programs, and collaborative research institutes (Wildavsky 2012; Altbach 2013; Knight 2013; Marginson 2015). University partnerships with common goals and shared resources are viewed as yielding advantages for strengthening capacity and innovation (van der Wende 2001; Pan 2009). Combining institutional cultures through academic mobility produces hybrid institutions expected to develop innovative approaches to knowledge creation and exchange (Cummings, Teichler, and Arimoto 2013; Tierney and Lanford 2015).

CHINESE-FOREIGN COOPERATION IN RUNNING SCHOOLS

Nevertheless, there are many obstacles that challenge the success of cross-system university partnerships. These include such matters as financial viability, currency convertibility, student recruitment, staff commitment, common language medium, and differences with respect to academic values or gender equity. While university partnerships are not a panacea, there are many notable successes. The European experience suggests that cross-national programs across adjacent systems with different language traditions can operate effectively and take advantage of cultural diversity. In East Asia, historical issues can be a hindrance to partnerships, but decades of building partnerships with Western universities have shifted more toward Asian intraregional cross-system partnerships.

EASTERN ASIA'S CROSS-BORDER PARTNERSHIPS IN HIGHER EDUCATION

Cross-system partnerships in Asia are gradually increasing and as part of a strategy for strengthening higher education institutions to play a more central role in the social and economic development of their countries (Huang 2006; Fegan and Field 2009; Pan 2009; Chapman, Cummings, and Postiglione 2010; Chapman and Sakamoto 2011). Research by the Asian Development Bank has pointed to a number of trends. (1) Partnerships often involve educators negotiating agreements, designing programs, and delivering services in settings and work contexts that are not fully familiar to them. (2) When partners believe they are gaining from the transaction, the partnering institutional leaders may not be valuing the aspects of the arrangement in the same way. (3) Even when both partners see the arrangements as beneficial, collaborators may have different motivations for participation, assess the value of activities in different ways, seek different outcomes, and value the same outcomes differently. (4) Greater complexity in cross-border collaborations can yield unanticipated consequences and governance challenges. (5) Cross-border collaborations require a long-term governance strategy because there is no quick return on investment. The most successful collaborations are initiated by individual academics through bottom-up strategies. However, as governments become more aware of the benefits of partnerships, initiatives increasingly rest with senior institutional leaders (Asian Development Bank 2012).

In short, the benefits of cross-border academic governance can be significant, but cannot be assumed. Much depends on roles and resources and how these partnerships are governed. Yet, done well, such partnerships provide a significant source of innovative thinking and creative sharing. The Asian cross-system experience contributes to the key theoretical issues at the center of debate in comparative higher education, such as the extent to which governance models became more similar or retain distinctive differences over the course of modernization and globalization.

From a neoinstitutional perspective, organizations and their form of governance are shaped by values in their environments (Meyer and Rowan 1977; DiMaggio and Powell 1983). In practice, they are compelled to become more alike in structures and roles, in standards, rules, and practices. Yet, organizations differ by roots, roles and resources. Therefore, there are bound to be both institutional isomorphism and loose coupling. Still, neoinstitutionalism points us in the direction of world models of organizational governance. In reality, university partnerships could not function without some degree of institutional isomorphism (Meyer and Ramirez 2007). But a key question is what a globalized environment means for making diversity more salient. Global rankings, best practices, educational hubs, cross-border partnerships, and other symbols of progress are often at odds with historically rooted models of a society or nation. The globalized environment also creates new rules of the game for the universities (Ramirez 2006, 2010).

Universities have social and cultural histories that influence their norms and values (Thelen 1999). This creates a path dependency that matters in how institutions evolve within changing environments (Selznick 1957; Thelen and Steinmo 1992; Christensen and Peters 1999; Pierson 2004; Peters 2011). Historical legacies carve paths for universities. This explains persistent differences in governance practices, as well as resistance to changes (Stinchcombe 1965). Thus, universities become reform-resistant when it involves cultural heritage (Brunsson and Olsen 1993). Selective reforms may become pragmatically adapted to fit a cultural heritage, and result in a new route to intended aims. A key issue concerns how universities continue to maintain their cultural roots over time and adapt to a new environment of institutional rules.

THE VALUE OF CASE STUDIES

Case studies can examine various motivations, goals, mechanisms, outcomes, and challenges associated with the governance of cross-border collaboration in higher education. In practical terms, outcomes are not always consistent with the motives and anticipated benefits, but effective governance of university partnerships can offer a useful strategy for capacity development, yield social and economic benefits, and enrich the academic experience of students. In theoretical terms, the rise of Asian universities, regional cooperation, and cross-border higher education have reinvigorated the study of comparative education systems by providing an opportunity to reconsider key issues such as the extent to which cross-border sharing makes higher education systems and institutions more similar or distinctly unique, more dependent or autonomous, and more or less nationally relevant in the course of globalization. Finally, case studies provide clear directions to further research into how governance of university partnerships can more successfully address the main challenges of economic globalization and deepen the dialogue among members of the global academy.

Evidences will be drawn from Chinese mainland and Hong Kong. The methods of data collection include document analysis, interviews, and observations. Documentary analysis included official government documents, such as regulations, and statistics in Chinese mainland and Hong Kong. Other documents come from the universities (e.g., the official websites, published reports, and statistics). Preliminary interviews were conducted with different stakeholders, including the students, teachers and administrators.

CHINA'S TWO-SYSTEM CASE STUDY

China's cross-system engagement with overseas partners in higher education has grown rapidly. The 2003 law on educational joint ventures opened the floodgates to hundreds of partnerships between Chinese and foreign universities (including those in the Hong Kong Special Administrative Region of China). For example, reforms are underway at top Chinese colleges to adapt and innovate on Western models of liberal arts higher education. Attention is building about whether foreign-partnership campuses can have a significant impact on

China's higher-education system. These collaborations and partnerships constitute one type of laboratory for innovative and, while the jury remains out on long term sustainability of cross-border campuses, both host and guest universities learn a great deal from cooperation in the running of partnered colleges and universities (Wildavsky 2012).

The majority of Sino-foreign partnership programs are taught and run by foreign academics, at a substantial premium, within Chinese universities (Pan 2009). In a few cases, foreign universities have gone one step further and set up full campuses in China. Nottingham University has a campus in Ningbo; Liverpool has established a university in Suzhou. In 2013, New York University, which already has overseas study programs in 10 countries, opened a new campus in Shanghai and will conduct integrated classes in humanities and social sciences, with an equal number of Chinese and foreign students. Duke University has also established a campus in Kunshan (Redden 2008). Others American universities with similar aspirations include Kean University and University of Montana (Redden 2014). Each of these universities cannot establish fully independent campuses on Chinese soil. Each has a host university. However, their degree of institutional autonomy has gradually increased year by year.

The rise in Sino-foreign joint ventures has led to more discussion about educational sovereignty. An influential scholar of Chinese higher education cautions that permitting foreign entities to hold a majority (more than 51%) of institutional ownership can lead to an "infiltration of Western values and cultures at odds with current Chinese circumstances" (Pan 2009, 90). Such views are important in the Chinese mainland (Zhang 2009a; Zhang 2009b). The education sovereignty issue has obvious implications for the Hong Kong campuses because Hong Kong has many Westernized universities. This offers a unique perspective on cross border campuses.

HONG KONG'S CROSS-SYSTEM COLLABORATION

Hong Kong is a special case because it is part of China. However, China's law on Sino-foreign cooperation in the running of educational institutions applies to Hong Kong. Hong Kong is not only able to hire talented academics globally but has a special attraction for some overseas and mainland Chinese academics, who can live in a Chinese environment, while at the same time enjoying working conditions like those at overseas universities.

What mainly distinguishes the university governance in Hong Kong is a high degree of institutional autonomy and academic freedom. This goes a long way to account for why most of Hong Kong's universities are in the world's top 200 according to the Times Higher Education. Hong Kong achieves this with a mere 0.7% of gross domestic product for R&D (about 50th in the world) but it sustains such a ranking due largely to the grit of their academic staff. Personnel matters and resource allocations are largely perceived by academic staff to be made on the basis of performance measures.

HISTORICAL BACKGROUND

Academic contact between universities in Hong Kong and the Chinese mainland has a long history. Hong Kong has long been a hub for Chinese higher education. The first Chinese to study in America (Yung Wing) attended Hong Kong's Morrison Education Society School before earning a degree from Yale University in 1854 (Ting and Pan 2003). The first group China sent to America in 1872 included Chow Shouson, Liang Tun Yen, and others who had attended school in Hong Kong. Dr. Sun Yat-sen, the Father of Modern China studied at the Hong Kong Medical College (later becoming The University of Hong Kong). The University of Hong Kong (HKU), established by the colonial government in 1911, aimed to help the modernization of China. Its first students were recruited from China and its overseas communities in Malaya (current Malaysia) and elsewhere.

The 40 years of economic reform and opening to the outside world on the Chinese mainland that began in 1978 had a significant effect on Hong Kong's long held position as the key bridging center for educational exchange with the West. To survive, Hong Kong adapted to changes on the Chinese mainland. The earlier role as a bridge contributed to the impetus for readapting as an international center for educational exchange. Hong Kong's cross-cultural sophistication and easy access to mainland sources permitted it to provide broad perspectives, reliable advice, and penetrating analyses of China's university reforms. This role has since become integrated with Hong Kong's transition to a knowledge economy and came to represent the nucleus of its vision for cross-system partnerships in higher education.

Before 1990, most degree courses were offered in the two universities, HKU and The Chinese University of Hong Kong (CUHK). A third university, the Hong Kong University of Science and Technology (HKUST), was established in 1991. The Hong Kong Polytechnic University (PolyU), the City University of Hong Kong (CityU), and the Hong Kong Baptist University (BaptistU) earned university status in 1994. Lingnan University was elevated to university status shortly afterward at the close of the colonial era (University Grants Committee 2002). The Education University of Hong Kong received university status in 2016. Hong Kong has a fully private Shue Yan University, as well as a government initiated self-funded Open University.

The contemporary university in Hong Kong is based on a Western model (Altbach 1997). It has continued to thrive because it plays a key role in economic and social development, engages in global academic discourse that contributes to the creation of new knowledge, and provides enduring ingredients for a genuine global culture (Wu 1992). Higher education in Hong Kong has had to adapt quickly to both the national and global environment. It has done this through expansion, internationalization, and cross-system educational exchanges, both international and with other parts of China.

Mok (2005) argued that the role of Hong Kong government and higher education governance has changed through adopting policies and strategies to promote entrepreneurial spirit and practices (e.g., by encouraging academic staff to venture in industrial, business, and commercial activities). Various funding schemes, such as the Applied Research Fund, Innovation and Technology Fund, have brought government, the private sector and higher education sector together in promoting entrepreneurial endeavors. The role of Hong Kong government has been a facilitator or an enabler in fostering entrepreneurship. Another key driver for change in academic governance is the proliferation of transnational educational programs. New governance and regulatory models have been adopted to address the issues of coordination, accountability, and transparency (Mok 2011; Mok and Ong 2012). At the same time, growing prominence of privatization in higher education has challenged the conventional education governance models. Mok (2008) explained how the Hong Kong government performs the role of a market facilitator instead of a market generator. Its primary focus is on quality assurance of these programs

CHINESE-FOREIGN COOPERATION IN RUNNING SCHOOLS

through providing sufficient information for the consumers (students) in Hong Kong to choose. On the other hand, the government has not taken an active role to facilitate universities in Hong Kong to develop joint programs in the Chinese mainland, nor has it encourage the setting up of joint centers or campuses.

Hong Kong's reunion with the Chinese mainland in 1997 further deepened contact and generated a new level of intersystem vitality. By 2015, Hong Kong's future had become increasingly dependent on the economy of the Chinese mainland and relations between Hong Kong and the Chinese mainland grew closer, despite controversies over the method of election of Hong Kong's Chief Executive.

THIRTY-FIVE YEARS OF ACADEMIC COOPERATION

Academic partnership program collaboration between higher education institutions in Hong Kong and the Chinese mainland began years before the resumption of sovereignty in 1997. In 1987, Hong Kong Shue Yan College (now University) and Peking University (PKU) launched a joint bachelor of law degree in Hong Kong. PKU professors delivered lectures in Hong Kong and graduates obtained a degree conferred by PKU. In May 1991, Shue Yan College established four part-time master's degree programs with PKU in Chinese classic literature, Chinese economy, international law, and civil law. A master degree in journalism was offered at Shue Yan College by Renmin University beginning in 1993.[1] These degree programs were approved by the State Education Commission (SEC) of China (formerly and currently the Ministry of Education in 1998). Following the SEC's "Interim Provisions for Sino-Foreign Cooperation in the running of educational institutions" (中外合作辦學暫行規定) in 1995, other universities in Hong Kong began to establish joint academic programs with their counterparts on the Chinese mainland.

HKU established an International MBA with Shanghai's Fudan University in 1998. PolyU offered a master of science in quality management with Hangzhou's Zhejiang University in 1999. CUHK offered an MBA in Finance with Tsinghua University's campuses in both Beijing and Shenzhen in 2000. These programs continue. Another early example of an HK-Mainland joint program of study is the Cheung Kong Graduate School of Business (長江商學院) launched by Hong Kong tycoon Li Ka Shing through his foundation in 2002 which considers itself as a private, nonprofit, independent educational institution and the only business school in Mainland China with faculty governance.[2]

The 2003 Law on Sino-Foreign cooperation in the running of educational institutions (中華人民共和國中外合作辦學條例) applies to institutions from Hong Kong SAR, Macau SAR, and Taiwan when undertaking collaborations with their mainland partners. The law further specifies that foreign institutions cannot establish independent programs and/or campuses. The two main types of partnership are (1) program collaboration and (2) joint campuses. We briefly review the programs but focus on a case study of a joint campus.

PROGRAM-LEVEL COLLABORATION

Hong Kong's universities have partnered with Mainland Chinese institutions in offering a wide variety of joint programs, many conducted in the campuses of the local partnering

CHINESE-FOREIGN COOPERATION IN RUNNING SCHOOLS

TABLE 1
Distribution of Degree Programs Offered by Hong Kong Universities (2014)

Program	HKU	CUHK	PolyU	HKUST	CityU	BaptistU	Total
Bachelor	1	0	2	0	1	0	4
Master	6	7	17	1	0	0	31
Doctorate	0	0	2	0	1	1	4
Total	7	7	21	1	2	1	39

universities. Some are offered in outposts or regional bases set up with the support from the local universities. In total, there are 39 commissioned programs (as shown in Table 1), of which there are four bachelor and four doctoral programs. The remaining 31 are master degree programs.

Although it did not establish a mainland campus, PolyU has established 21 of Hong Kong's 39 joint programs in the Chinese mainland, largely at regional bases[3] (Zhejiang University in Hangzhou, Xi'an University in Xi'an, Sichuan University in Chengdu, East China University of Science and Technology in Shanghai), as shown in Table 2. Most of these master programs are part-time and targeted at participants who have working experiences in various industries or sectors.

TABLE 2
Chinese Partnering Universities by Location of Program

Location	Hong Kong's partnering institutes on the mainland	Bachelor degree	Master degree	Doctorate degree	Total
Beijing	Tsinghua University	0	1	0	1
	Peking University	0	2	0	2
	Renmin University of China	0	1	1	2
	Chinese Academy of Science	0	2	0	2
Tianjin	Nankai University	0	1	1	2
Shanghai	Fudan University	0	3	1	4
	Shanghai National Accounting Institute	0	1	0	1
	East China University of Political Science & Law	1	0	0	1
	East China University of Science & Technology	0	1	0	1
Hangzhou	Zhejiang University	1	4	1	6
Xi'an	Xi'an Jiaotong University	1	3	0	4
	Xi'an Polytechnic University	0	1	0	1
Chengdu	Sichuan University	0	4	0	4
Chongqing	Chongqing University	0	2	0	2
Guangzhou	Sun Yat-sen University	1	0	0	1
Shenzhen	Tsinghua University	0	2	0	2
	Peking University	0	3	0	3
Total		4	31	4	39

JOINT CAMPUSES

Joint campuses provide an opportunity to examine aspects of institutional governance and academic culture. Three Hong Kong universities have established joint campuses loosely coupled to a mainland partner university. However, two cases have only been in operation for less than two years. The third one has operated for over a decade and provides a useful case for examining university partnership between Hong Kong and the Chinese mainland. We will briefly review the first two joint campuses and focus on the third one.

Chinese University of Hong Kong-Shenzhen

Chinese University of Hong Kong-Shenzhen (CUHK-SZ; 香港中文大学 (深圳) was established in 2014 by CUHK and Shenzhen University (SZU). It is conceived as an extension or branch campus of CUHK with a vision to become a first-class research university regionally, nationally and internationally.[4] It plans 23 undergraduate degree programs within three schools (management and economics, science and engineering, humanities, and social sciences). CUHK-SZ promotes itself as providing research-based teaching. In the academic year 2014–15, it enrolled 313 undergraduates. It aims to recruit most students from the Chinese mainland's 17 provincial level entities, as well as some international students. The graduates will be awarded both the CUHK-SZ Graduation Certificate and the CUHK Degree. The medium of instruction will be both Chinese and English, as is the practice at CUHK. The Governing Board is chaired by the vice-chancellor of CUHK. The Board comprises of sixteen members, eight respectively nominated by CUHK and SZU. The president of CUHK-SZ is also a member of CUHK. It appears that SZU's influence in this campus is not prominent. It is more like a branch campus of CUHK than a joint institute of CUHK and SZU.

HKUST Joint School of Sustainable Development

In 2014, HKUST and Xian-Jiaotong University (XJTU) established a XJTU-HKUST Joint School of Sustainable Development (JSSD; 西安交大-香港科大可持續發展學院).[5] JSSD is a nonprofit and jointly run institution. Instead of building a new campus, JSSD is located within the campus of XJTU. It has similar functions as other schools in both universities, including undergraduate and postgraduate education, academic research and technology innovation. JSSD plans to recruit 60 students per major each year for undergraduate programs, twenty students per major each year for master programs, and 15 students per major each year for doctorate programs. Undergraduates will be conferred dual bachelor degrees of XJTU and HKUST; postgraduate students will be conferred dual master or dual doctorate degrees of XJTU and HKUST. JSSD adopts an education model featuring exploratory institutional mechanisms to introduce HKUST's resources such as its teaching materials, syllabus systems, and instructional methods. It uses English as the medium of instruction for all classroom lectures. JSSD employs a group of tenured professors from HKUST (with more than 10 years of teaching experience) for teaching. They also serve as course group leaders to take charge of course importation, transformation, value-addition and innovation. Furthermore, they are responsible for setting up course plans and monitoring the teaching quality.

Hong Kong-Mainland Joint-University X[6]

The first Hong Kong-Mainland China university partnership was established in 2005, between university from Hong Kong (hereinafter referred to as UH) and a university from the Mainland (hereinafter referred to as UM); the resulting new institution (hereinafter referred to as UX) is located in South China. Promoted as "a new liberal arts college serving China and the world,"[7] its vision is to "create an innovative international education model for China that can contribute to the welfare of the nation and the world."[8] Its mission is to "build a new model for liberal education in mainland China and to nurture talented future graduates with international perspectives."[9] As of 2015, UX offered 20 bachelor degree programs, divided among three college divisions: business and management; humanities and social sciences; and science and technology.

Most students in UX are recruited from the Chinese mainland on the basis of their National College and University Entrance Examinations scores; however, students from the home province in which UX is located are assessed for admission based on their National College and University Entrance Examination scores (60%), UX entrance tests (30%), and senior middle school academic performance (10%). To encourage diversity and internationalization, UX also admits students from Hong Kong, Macau, Taiwan, and overseas.[10] Graduates are awarded a degree of UH, and a Graduate Certificate of UX. English is the language of instruction at UX.

Governance of UX

The main legislative implement addressing cross-border higher education cooperation in China is the Regulations of the People's Republic of China on Chinese-foreign Cooperation in Running Schools (State Council 2003), which govern "cooperative education conducted by the education institutions from Hong Kong, Macao Special Administrative Region and Taiwan area and the education institutions of the mainland of China."[11] As currently there are no specific policy documents on cooperative education between Hong Kong and mainland China, the 2003 Law also sets out the legal framework for higher education cooperation between the two regions.

UX was established soon after the promulgation of the 2003 Law. To fulfill the requirement of its legal framework,[12] UX set up a Council[13] of 10 members—five from UH and five from UM. UX's current President (a past president from UH) is responsible for the management of UX. During the founding stage of UX, the Council Chair and the President played essential roles in initiating cooperation between UH and UM.

Interorganizational Interactions

Compared to the role of UM, UH's influence on UX is more prominent. The current President of UX worked at UH for many years, including 9 years as its president.[14] This laid a solid foundation for interorganizational relations between UH and UX; for instance, the organizational form of committee structure common in academic governance at Hong Kong universities is employed at UX.[15] The curriculum and programs are tailored to the needs of mainland Chinese students based on the practices in UH and other Hong Kong universities, and UH's "whole personal education" approach has been adopted by and revised for UX.[16] Eight modules (adversity management, environmental awareness, emotional intelligence, experiential arts, experiential development, sports culture, university life, and voluntary service) have been identified, and a series of courses based on an experiential learning approach are offered at UX.[17]

Hall education and hall culture, which are common elements of Hong Kong colleges and universities, are also emphasized at UX[18]; each hall has a name, a students' association, and hall tutors; and interhall competitions, high table dinners, and hall day forums are held from time to time. Each summer, UX students are given the opportunity to attend summer programs at UH and earn credits that are transferable to UX.[19] Two graduation ceremonies are held annually—one in June at UX, at which graduates receive their certification,[20] and the other in November at UH, at which graduates receive their degree.[21] As UX students' degrees are issued by UH, the external examiner system and advisory committees[20] common in Hong Kong universities have been established gradually at UX,[22] and HKBU conducts periodic institutional reviews to ensure UX maintains expected academic standards.[23] UX also employs UH's traditional honorary fellowship system.[24]

The observed interrelations between UX and UH are consistent with the hypothesis (proposed by institutional theorists) that the greater the dependence of one organization on another is, the more similar the former will become to the latter in terms of structure, climate, and behavioral focus (DiMaggio and Powell 1983). In this case, examples of institutional isomorphism can be found in UX's imitation of UH's operation and governance, including its council and committee structure, curriculum design, student administration, and organizational reviews.

Interactions Between Organization and Environment

As institutional theorists have emphasized, "environments constitute local situations" (Meyer and Ramirez 2007), and universities, as organizational actors, are therefore shaped by their wider environment. Unlike UH, which is rooted deeply in the cultural and historical conditions of Hong Kong society, UX has had to adapt to the characteristics and practices of mainland Chinese society. Moreover, UX's interactions with external mainland Chinese social and cultural contexts vividly prove institutional theorists' assertions that "organizations that incorporate societally legitimated rationalized elements in their formal structures maximize their legitimacy and increase their resources and survival capabilities" (Meyer and Rowan 1977).

During its 10 years of development, UX evolved gradually under the influence of the wider environments by adopting various coping strategies. For instance, due to the combined effects of mainland China's family planning policies and the emergence (since the 1978 implementation of China's Open Door Policy) of a Chinese middle class (Tsang 2013), a large number of students enrolled in UX are only children from relatively affluent families; moreover, due to the twin impacts of Confucian tradition (which values the role of education plays in social mobility) and neoliberalism (which considers education a commodity or service), Chinese middle class parents pay close attention to their children's performance at school and university. This is especially true for UX, a newly established college that relies heavily on tuition fees for its operation, particularly at this early stage of existence. As a result, a special administrative team, named the "Parental Affairs Section,"[24] was established as part of UX's "Four-point Education Coordination Office"[27] to manage the university's relationship with parents by updating them on students' performance and progress, explaining university regulations and policies, answering parents' questions, and coordinating parents' support for its efforts at cultivating and educating students. Compared to universities in both Hong Kong and mainland China, this organizational characteristic is unusual, and mirrors the wider social context and background of the Chinese society of which UX is a part.

This is also reflected in UX's evolving relationship with local and central governments. For instance, to fulfill mainland government requirements, UX—like most other mainland Chinese universities—offers military training to its freshmen,[28] albeit only for one week; this practice does not exist in Hong Kong universities. In addition, a Communist Party Committee, a common feature of most mainland Chinese universities, has been gradually established at UX,[28] although it does not play a leading role. Through these loosely decoupled mechanisms (Weick 1976), UX is learning to adapt to the wider environment, and is gaining organizational legitimacy in mainland China. It is notable that, in 2014, the Zhuhai government approved the allocation of an additional 200 mu (33 acres) of land for a new UX campus,[29] a move vital to the university's expansion and further development. This remarkable event could be viewed as a signal that UX has further improved its relationship with the local government, thus gaining more resources to allow it prosper. However, the relationship between an organization and its environment is bidirectional; UX has also slowly begun to influence its surroundings (locally, nationally, and globally), largely through the actions of its graduates.

To sum up, as current UX President Ng Ching-Fai has emphasized, "as the first Hong Kong–mainland university partnership, [and] the first experiment of building a liberal arts college in mainland [China],"[30] UX is a pioneer in bringing the Hong Kong model of higher education to mainland China. Its unique organizational features—such as its committee structure, international perspective, whole-person education model, hall education mode, and quality assurance system (Zee 2015)—are innovative departures from traditional Chinese higher education, and provide more options to Chinese students, in particular those from middle-class mainland Chinese families. The establishment of UX can be conceptualized as a process of institutional adaptation, and as a valuable means of exploring how, why, and to what extent the Hong Kong model of academic organization is applicable on the mainland. In the case of UX, some elements of the Hong Kong model have been retained, while others have gradually changed due to the influence of the wider environment. Further research is needed to investigate which elements have been kept, added, deleted, or changed, to what extent, and for what reasons.

GOVERNING OF HONG KONG HIGHER EDUCATION PROGRAMS IN THE CHINESE MAINLAND

There has been a growing popularity among Hong Kong's universities to establish a cross-border presence on the Chinese mainland. This is due to the deepening relations between the two systems, the perceived need to fill program niches in certain curriculum areas, the international flavor of the Hong Kong programs, and the opportunity to make their university brands more salient on the Chinese mainland. Nevertheless, there are challenges in establishing models of governance that maintain Hong Kong more bottom-up governance style.

Hong Kong's cross-border partnerships on the Chinese mainland have helped to improve instructional delivery by their emphasis on soft skills and liberal arts education curriculum, as well as the offering of niche programs. However, improvements in research capacity in science and technology have come in other ways, through cross-border research institutes and other joint collaboration projects at state laboratories. Most programs were initially established in the adjoining region of Guangdong province, especially in the economic zones of Shenzhen and Zhuhai. However, more Hong Kong cross-border programs are now offered at universities elsewhere on the Chinese mainland.

Governance of Hong Kong programs in the Chinese mainland requires adaptations to the more top-down format of mainland university governance, although there is room to retain aspects of the Hong Kong universities' learning ethos, including the emphasis on liberal studies. Hong Kong programs most in demand are short-term master degree programs in professional areas of study offered in part-time mode. These permit Hong Kong programs to fill a niche in mainland higher education program offerings in ways that are cost effective for Hong Kong's universities. Some mainland students view these programs as providing possible job opportunities in both systems.

Hong Kong degree programs on the Chinese mainland differ from those of the main foreign campuses such as Nottingham-Ningbo, NYU-Shanghai, and Duke University-Kunshan in one key respect. Hong Kong cross-border programs generally do not aim to bring students from the two systems together to live and attend class together, conduct project-based collaboration, and study together. It may be caused by the facts that most of these are part-time master programs in professional areas.

Finally, Hong Kong cross-border programs on the Chinese mainland have a greater risk potential. The domestic brand of overseas university would be much less affected by its Chinese campus than would the domestic brand of Hong Kong campuses. In short, the brand of universities in Hong Kong is more easily affected by their mainland campuses. However, there are also advantages. Unlike overseas academics, who lose time on their research programs by having to travel long distances to their China-based campus, Hong Kong academics can arrive in the Chinese mainland to teach and return to their research in Hong Kong campuses within the same day. The common similarity of cross-border programs from Hong Kong and overseas is their peripheral position within the larger system of Chinese higher education.

NOTES

1. Website of Shun Yan College: www.hksyu.edu/Info/cooperation_china.html.
2. Website of Cheung Kong Graduate School of Business: http://english.ckgsb.edu.cn/content/next-generation-business-school.
3. Hong Kong Polytechnic University. 2015. Regional bases with specialized focuses. http://www.polyu.edu.hk/cmao/eng/?p=regional-bases.
4. The Chinese University of Hong Kong, Shenzhen. 2015. Mission and vision. http://www.cuhk.edu.cn/en/About/index183.html.
5. JSSD, XJTU-HKUST Joint School of Sustainable Development. 2015. Introduction. http://jssd.xjtu.edu.cn/en/page/content/1/1?p_menu=1.
6. The name of the university is anonymized due to ethical considerations.
7. Mission and vision. 2012. Retrieved from the official website of UX, accessed May 20, 2016.
8. Mission and vision. 2012. Retrieved from the official website of UX, accessed May 20, 2016.
9. Mission and vision. 2012. Retrieved from the official website of UX, accessed May 20, 2016.
10. Admission policies. 2015. Retrieved from the official website of UX, accessed May 20, 2016.
11. According to Article 59, "Cooperation in running schools between educational institutions from the Hong Kong Special Administrative Region, the Macao Special Administrative Region or Taiwan and mainland educational

CHINESE-FOREIGN COOPERATION IN RUNNING SCHOOLS

institutions shall be handled with reference to the provisions of these Regulations." http://www.moe.edu.cn/publicfiles/business/htmlfiles/moe/moe_861/200506/8646.html

12. According to Article 21, "A Chinese-foreign cooperatively-run school with the legal person status shall set up a board of trustees or a board of directors"; and "Chinese members on the board of trustees, the board of directors or of the joint managerial committee shall not be less than half of the total number."

13. UX Council. 2015. Retrieved from the official website of UX, accessed May 20, 2016.

14. College administration. 2014. Retrieved from the official website of UX, accessed May 20, 2016.

15. Committee structure. 2015. Retrieved from the official website of UX, accessed May 20, 2016.

16. Guo, H. P. 2014–11. Whole person education: the soul of innovative liberal arts education in UX. Campus newsletter, issue 48, p. 4.

17. Zee, S. Y. 2015. UX: Liberal arts education in China. Beijing: China Renmin University Press, pp. 44, 77–78, 80.

18. Zee, S. Y. 2012. Build soft power in students' halls. Campus newsletter, issue 29, A6.

19. UX Hong Kong office. 2007. UX summer program at UH. Campus newsletter, Issue 6, B2C1

20. Chen, X. 2009. UX proudly presents the first graduating class of 2009. Campus newsletter, Issue 15, A1A2.

21. Wang, J. P. 2013. UX graduates are conferred UH degrees. Campus newsletter, issue 33, p. 4

22. Li, Z. Z. 2011. The First Advisory Committee in UX. Campus newsletter, issue 27, A6.

23. Chen, X. H. 2014. The 5th institutional review by UH. Campus newsletter, issue 43, p. 1.

24. UX Media and Public Relations Office. 2013. UX confers the first Honorary Fellowships on four prominent individuals. Campus newsletter, issue 37, p. 1.

25. The Parents Section. Retrieved from official website of UX, accessed May 20, 2016.

26. "Four Point Education" is an education model invented by UX. Students are in the center; surrounded by teachers and college, parents, and society working together to cultivate the students.

27. Tong, H. Y. 2013. Different "military training" in UX. Campus newsletter, issue 34, p. 4.

28. Chen, X. H. 2011. UX committee of Communist Party of China launches its inaugural meeting. Campus newsletter, issue 28, A4.

29. Yu, Y. Y. 2014. New cooperation with government, new campus at groundbreaking. Campus newsletter, issue 46, p. 1.

30. Chen, X. H. 2015. New decade, new challenges for UX. Campus newsletter, issue 55, p. 1.

FUNDING

This work was supported by the Research Grants Council (HKU37600514, HKU7021-PPR-12).

REFERENCES

Asian Development Bank. 2012. *Higher education across Asia: Issues and strategies*. Manila: ADB.

Altbach, P. G. 1997. *Comparative higher education: Knowledge, the university, and development*. Boston: Center for International Higher Education.

Altbach, P. G. 2013. *The Asian higher education century? The international imperative in higher education*, 143–47. Rotterdam, the Netherlands: Sense.

Brunsson, N., and J. P. Olsen. 1993. *The reforming organization*. London: Routledge.

Chapman, D. W., W. K. Cummings, and G. A. Postiglione. 2010. *Crossing borders in East Asia higher education*. New York: Springer Press.

Chapman, D. W., and R. Sakamoto. 2011. *Cross-border partnerships in higher education: Strategies and issues*. London: Routledge.

Christensen, T., and B. G. Peters. 1999. *Structure, culture and governance: A comparative analysis of Norway and the United States*. Lanham, MD: Rowman and Littlefield.

Cummings, W. K., U. Teichler, and A. Arimoto. 2013. *The changing academic profession—Major findings of a comparative survey*. New York: Springer.

DiMaggio, P. J., and W. W. Powell. 1983. The iron cage revisited: Institutional isomorphism and collective rationality in organizational fields. *American Sociological Review* 48:147–60. doi:10.2307/2095101

CHINESE-FOREIGN COOPERATION IN RUNNING SCHOOLS

Fegan, J., and M. H. Field. 2009. *Education across borders: politics, policy and legislative action*. New York: Springer.

Huang, F. 2006. Transnational higher education in mainland China: A focus on foreign degree-conferring programs In *Transnational higher education in Asia and the Pacific Region*, ed. F. Huang 21–33. Hiroshima: Research Institute for Higher Education, Hiroshima University.

Knight, J. 2013. The changing landscape of higher education internationalisation—for better or worse? *Perspectives: Policy and Practice in Higher Education* 17 (3):84–90.

Maoyuan, P. 2009. China's international partnerships and cross-border cooperation. *Chinese Education and Society* 42 (4):88–96. doi:10.2753/CED1061-1932420400

Marginson, S. 2015. The strategy positioning of Australian research universities in the East region. *Higher Education* 70 (2):265–81. doi:10.1007/s10734-014-9839-5

Meyer, J. W., and F. O. Ramirez. 2007. Higher education as institution. In *Sociology of higher education: Contributions and their contexts*, ed. P. J. Gumport. Baltimore: The Johns Hopkins University Press.

Meyer, J. W., and B. Rowan. 1977. Institutionalized organizations: Formal structure as myth and ceremony. *American Journal of Sociology* 83:340–63. doi:10.1086/226550

Mok, K. H. 2005. Fostering entrepreneurship: Changing role of government and higher education governance in Hong Kong. *Research Policy* 34:537–55. doi:10.1016/j.respol.2005.03.003

Mok, K. H. 2008. Varieties of regulatory regimes in Asia: The liberalization of the higher education market and changing governance in Hong Kong, Singapore and Malaysia. *Pacific Review* 21:147–70. doi:10.1080/09512740801990220

Mok, K. H. 2011. Regional responses to globalization challenges: The assertion of soft power and changing university governance in Singapore, Hong Kong and Malaysia. In *Handbook on globalization and higher education*, ed. R. King S. Marginson, and R. Naidoo, 179–96. Northampton, MA: Edward Elgar.

Mok, K. H., and K. C. Ong. 2012. Asserting brain power and expanding education services: searching for new governance and regulatory regimes in Singapore and Hong Kong. In *The emergent knowledge society and the future of higher education: Asian perspectives*, ed. D. Neubauer 139–60. New York: Routledge.

Pan, M. Y. 2009. An analytical differentiation of the relationship between education sovereignty and education rights. *Chinese Education and Society* 42 (4):88–96. doi:10.2753/CED1061-1932420407

Peters, B. 2011. *Institutional theory in political science: The new institutionalism*. New York: Continuum.

Pierson, P. 2004. *Politics in time: History, institutions, and social analysis*. New Haven, CT: Yale University Press.

Ramirez, F. O. 2006. The rationalization of the university. In *Transnational governance: Institutional dynamics of regulation* ed. M. L. Dejelic, and K. Sahlin-Anderson. Cambridge: Cambridge University Press.

Ramirez, F. O. 2010. Accounting for excellence: Transforming universities into organizational actors. In *Higher education, policy, and the global competition phenomenon*, ed. V. Rust, L. Portnoi, and S. Bagely. London: Palgrave.

Redden, E. 2008. Bucking the branch campus. Inside higher education. March 12. Retrieved 30 June 2014. http://www.insidehighered.com/news/2014/03/12/amid-branch-campus-building-boom-some-universities-reject-model#ixzz34fcVHp8L.

Redden, E. 2014. Phantom campus in China. Inside higher education. February 12. Retrieved 30 June 2014. http://www.insidehighered.com/news/2008/02/12/china#sthash. XjQmRUiI.dpbs.

Selznick, P. 1957. *Leadership in administration: A sociological interpretation*. New York: Harper and Row.

State Council. 2003. *Regulations of the People's Republic of China on Chinese-Foreign Cooperation in Running Schools （中华人民共和国中外合作办学条例）*. http://www.moe.edu.cn/publicfiles/business/htmlfiles/moe/moe_861/200506/8646.html

Stinchcombe, A. L. 1965. Social structure and organizations. In *Handbook of organizations*, ed. J. G. March 142–93. Chicago: Rand McNally.

Thelen, K. 1999. Historical institutionalism in comparative politics. *Annual Review of Political Science* 2:369–404. doi:10.1146/annurev.polisci.2.1.369

Thelen, K., and S. Steinmo. 1992. Historical institutionalism in comparative politics. In *Structuring politics: Historical institutionalism in comparative politics*, ed. S. Steinmo K. A. Thelen, and F. Longstreth. New York: Cambridge University Press.

Tierney, W. G., and M. Lanford. 2015. An investigation of the impact of international branch campuses on organizational culture, *Higher Education* 70 (2):283–98. doi:10.1007/s10734-014-9845-7

Ting, J. S. P., and Z. Pan. 2003. *Boundless learning: Foreign educated students in modern China*. Hong Kong: Hong Kong History Museum.

Tsang, E. 2013. The quest for higher education by the Chinese middle class: Retrenching social mobility? *Higher Education* 66:653–68. doi:10.1007/s10734-013-9627-7

University Grants Committee. 2002. *Higher education in Hong Kong - Report of the University Grants Committee.* Hong Kong: Government Printer.

van der Wende, M. 2001. Internationalisation policies: about new trends and contrasting paradigms. *Higher Education Policy* 14 (3):249–59. doi:10.1016/S0952-8733(01)00018-6

Weick, K. E. 1976. Educational organizations as loosely coupled systems. *Administrative Science Quarterly* 21 (1):1–19. doi:10.2307/2391875

Wildavsky, B. 2012. *The great brain race: How global universities are reshaping the world.* Princeton: Princeton University Press.

Wu, W. G. 1992, November 22–24. The universities of the future: Roles in the changing world order. Paper presented at the first Richard A. Harville Conference on Higher Education, University of Arizona, Tucson.

Zee, S. Y. 2015. *UX: Liberal arts education in China.* Beijing: China Renmin University Press.

Zhang, L. 2009a. Policy direction and development trends for Sino-foreign partnership schools. *Chinese Education and Society* 42 (4):11–22. doi:10.2753/CED1061-1932420401

Zhang, M. X. 2009b. New era. new policy: Cross-border education and Sino-Foreign cooperation in running schools in the eyes of fence-sitter. *Chinese Education and Society* 42 (4):23–40. doi:10.2753/CED1061-1932420402

Cross-Border Higher Education in China: How the Field of Research Has Developed

Qin Yunyun and Alice Y.C. Te

Abstract: The aim of the research was to investigate how the field of cross-border Chinese higher education has developed from 1990 to 2015. Ninety-five articles in international journals and 470 articles in national journals were collected and analyzed in terms of authorship pattern, thematic clusters, and research methods. Results show that cross-border Chinese higher education has become an important topic in both the international and national academic community. In general, researchers from Mainland China and Hong Kong have dominated the field. Articles covering overviews, trends, and policy issues constituted the largest proportion of the total literature. However, students' experiences as a research focus is underrepresented in the current literature. The methods of document analysis and case study are used widely by the researchers. To see growth in the field, more collaboration between national researchers and international scholars is needed; so too are more empirical studies at the microlevel, particularly the experiences of students and teachers; and finally, more diversified and intensive research methods, for example longitudinal or ethnographic study, are suggested.

In recent years, cross-border education has become a global phenomenon. Knight (2007) defined cross-border education as the movement of people, programs, providers, curricula, projects, research, and services across national or regional jurisdictional borders. Among the various types of cross-border education, we focus on Sino-foreign cooperative education, which refers to the activities of launching education institutions (or programs), that mainly aim at enrolling Chinese citizens, by foreign education institutions and Chinese education institutions (jointly) within China (Chinese State Council 2006). In this research we focus on the cooperative activities at the higher education level.

Cross-border higher education is growing fast in China. China has become a flourishing country not only in exporting students overseas, but also in importing international education. According to data from the Chinese Ministry of Education (Ministry of Education 2013), around 550,000 Chinese students are currently enrolled in about 2,000 cross-border cooperative educational programs and institutes in Mainland China. About 450,000 students (or over 80%) are enrolled in joint programs or institutions at 577 universities and colleges, accounting for

CHINESE-FOREIGN COOPERATION IN RUNNING SCHOOLS

1.4% of the overall enrollment in Chinese higher education. Over 1.5 million Chinese college students have graduated from such joint programs or institutes. As a majority of these programs and students are in higher education, investigation is of the utmost importance.

As the practice of cross-border higher education in Mainland China continues to boom, a body of literature has emerged covering a wide range of themes and addressing various problems both in national and international journals. In these earlier literature reviews, few researchers have quantified the research on the topic and investigated the key features of the literature. For instance, in the national journals, only two papers (Tao and Shen 2006; Wang 2012) identified the major themes and features of existing literature on Sino-foreign cooperation in running schools at the higher education level. The biggest problem of these articles is that their analyses were based on literature written in Chinese alone, completely lacking data from international journals. Another article (Li and Jiang 2007) reviewed the Western literature on transnational higher education, however it was published in 2007 and more articles have since appeared in recent years. With regard to the international scholars, a recent study (Kosmützky and Putty 2016) conducted a systematic literature review on transnational, offshore, cross-border, and borderless education and captured 640 journal articles covering the years 2004–2014 in the Western research community. It is an indicator of the maturity of the thematic field. On top of providing descriptive analysis on the literature, it provides a review of the most recognized work in this thematic area. However, one of its limitations is the lack of Asian journals, as is the case in many western databases. Moreover, there is a paucity of literature reviews which focus on cross-border higher education in Mainland China. Another notable deficiency is that journal articles published in Chinese were usually omitted due to the language barrier. For these reasons, the previous research is insufficient, particularly in the data sources.

The aim of this research was to investigate how the field of "cross-border Chinese higher education research" has developed from 1990 to 2015 both in the national and international academic communities. The research questions this paper focuses on are: first, what is being researched and how the topic is researched in international journals and national journals? What are the main characteristics of the field? What are the differences between the publication patterns of international and national journals?

The main body of the article consists of three parts. The first section specifically illustrates the methodology of the research, including which databases were selected, what selection criteria was applied, and the time frame of the selection. The second section identifies the major features of the journal articles that were collected. They are then analyzed in terms of numbers, authorship patterns, thematic clusters, and research methods. For each part, comparisons are made between international journals and national journals. Finally, critics on the current research including theoretical orientations and methodological issues are provided, and possible directions for future research are discussed as well.

METHODOLOGY

To address the research questions, a total of 95 journals articles written in English and 470 journal articles in Chinese were collected and analyzed. For the English-language literature, using the search terms *China, Chinese (Sino) - foreign (UK/US/Canada/Australia)* and *cross (-)border education, transnational education, offshore education,* or *borderless education* that appear in titles, abstracts, or key terms, we searched all journal articles in Web of Science, ERIC, and SCOPUS that were published from 1990 to 2015. The search was limited to peer-reviewed journals published in English. Although in the key word search, the word *higher* education is not specified to have a broader search, the results indicate that all the articles identified were related to higher education.

In the first round of searches, we identified 31 articles in the Web of Science, 34 in ERIC, and 27 in SCOPUS. Some of these articles were overlapping, and the content of some articles were not relevant. For example, one article mentions *China* in the abstract as just an example, yet the article focused on other countries without any further elaboration relating to China. Eliminating the overlapping and irrelevant papers, there were 62 articles that remain. To capture a more comprehensive array of research studies not turned up by the initial search, two further steps were taken. First, we identified the quarterly publication of the Center for International Higher Education at the Boston College Center for International Higher Education, titled *International Higher Education*, as it captured the writings of distinguished international scholars including commentary and current information on key issues that shape international higher education. A total of 12 articles that discuss issues in relation to cross-border higher education in Mainland were found. Second, we identified and searched two journals with special emphasis on China education (i.e., *Frontiers of Education in China* and *Chinese Education and Society*). The same search terms were used in the search process. A total of 21 articles were identified. As a result, after the three rounds of searches, 95 articles were extracted and analyzed.

The Chinese literature comes from the China Academic Journals Full-text Database (CJFD) provided by the China National Knowledge Infrastructure (CNKI). In the CJFD, the keywords of *he zuo ban xue* (合作办学; English translation: cooperative education) were used for title searching and the results show that around 4,000 journal articles have been published. To guarantee the quality of the journal articles, we limited our analysis to the journal articles from the Chinese Social Sciences Citation Index (CSSCI), in which a total of 470 articles were collected and downloaded at the end of February 2016. For each article, the basic information including title, author(s), publication year, source, abstract, key words, and citation frequency were extracted and analyzed.

OVERVIEW OF THE DEVELOPMENT OF THE FIELD

Number of Journal Articles by Year

Figure 1 shows the number of articles published in international journals and national journals respectively from 1990 to 2016. Chronologically, there has been a steady growth of publications in international journals from 2004 onward. It reached its peak in 2009 when 16 articles were published. From 2012 onward there was a steady growth of publications. Four recently published articles in international journals in 2016 have been added to present a more comprehensive picture of the literature.

Similarly, the number of publications in national journals has increased consistently from 1990 to 2015. There have however, been some ups and downs during the period. 2003 can be seen as a watershed with 23 articles being published, before which the number of publications was relatively small. 2003 was also the year when *Regulations of the People's*

FIGURE 1 Number of journal articles in international journals and national journals.

Republic of China on Chinese-foreign Cooperative Education was issued by Chinese State Council. 2010 witnessed the peak of publication when 49 articles were published. In recent years, from 2010 to 2015, there has been another surge of publications.

Authorship Patterns

As shown in Table 1 below, of the 95 articles in international journals, 58 (61%) were published by single authors, and 37 (39%) were coauthored (two or more authors). For coauthored articles, 18 (49%) of them had coauthors from the same country, and 19 (51%) had coauthors from a different country. The country (or region) refers to the location of the affiliated institutions of the authors, instead of the nationality of the authors.

For articles published by a single author, Figure 2 shows that 13 of them were written by authors with affiliations to institutions in Mainland China, whereas 11 articles were written by authors from Hong Kong. Both categories constitute 41% of the single-authored articles. The other authors are mainly affiliated with institutions in the United States, Australia, and the United Kingdom, which are the common countries of Mainland China's cross-border partnership.

Of the 37 coauthored articles, 22 (around 60%) of them had coauthors from Mainland China, and 11 (30%) of them had coauthors from Hong Kong. The pattern is similar with single-authored articles, as Mainland China and Hong Kong constitute the major group of authors. Table 2 shows that for coauthorship between the same country (or region), Mainland China, Hong Kong, the United Kingdom, and Canada have a similar number of articles published. For coauthorship across countries (or regions), authors from Mainland China collaborated mainly with the United Kingdom, Canada or Australia. Mainland China, and Hong Kong still dominate, as there is relatively less collaboration between authors among foreign countries.

TABLE 1
Pattern of Authorship in International Journals

Number of articles			Coauthored articles	
Total	Single author	Coauthors	With coauthors in same countries	With coauthors in other countries
95	58 (61%)	37 (39%)	18 (49%)	19 (51%)

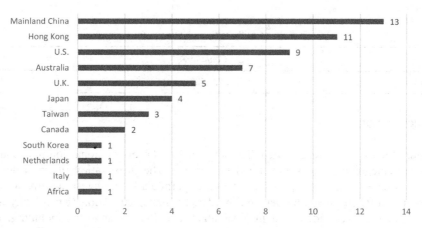

FIGURE 2 Single-authored publications in international journals, by authors' affiliation. Unit: Number of articles. Country (or region) refers to the location of the institutions affiliated to the authors. Hong Kong is a Special Administrative Region of China.

Considering the authorship of the national journal articles, 197 articles were written by a single author, and 273 articles were published by two or more authors, as shown in Table 3. Table 4 demonstrates the coauthorship pattern in national journals: the majority of scholars from Mainland China mainly coauthored with other authors in Mainland, rather than authors from other countries or regions.

TABLE 2
Coauthorship Pattern in International Journals: By authors' affiliation

	With authors from same countries/regions	
	Mainland China	5
	Hong Kong	3
	UK	4
	Canada	3
	Others	3
	Total	18
	With authors from other countries/regions	
Mainland China &	UK	3
	Canada	3
	Australia	3
	US	1
	Hong Kong	1
	South Korea	1
Hong Kong &	Australia	2
	UK	1
	US	1
Others	UK & Canada	3
	UK & Lithuania	
	US & Canada	
Total		19

Note. Other coauthorships in the same country (or region) include Macau, Belgium, and France.

CHINESE-FOREIGN COOPERATION IN RUNNING SCHOOLS

TABLE 3
Pattern of Authorship in National Journals

Single author	Coauthors	Total
197 (42%)	273 (58%)	470 (100%)

Thematic Clusters

The major themes of the research studies published in the international journals and national journals are categorized and summarized in Table 5. The justification of this categorization of themes is based mainly on previous literature, particularly the latest systematic review on transnational, offshore, cross-border, and borderless higher education (Kosmützky and Putty 2016). Six themes were identified in Kosmützky and Putty's analysis, including: overview and trends; quality assurance and regulation; teaching and learning; institutional and management perspectives; governance and policy, and student choice and student mobility. The most obvious deficiency of their review was that Asian journals were largely missing. In this research, the six themes listed previously were adopted as a benchmark for analysis, and new themes were added as driven by the characteristics of the data collected.

Of the 95 articles published in international journals, 21 articles (22%) of them analyzed the overview and trends for the emergence of cross-border higher education collaboration between Mainland China and other countries. Some of them traced the historical development, outlined the social and political context, identified the characteristics and concerns of the development, and positioned transnational higher education in Mainland China as an integral part of internationalization (e.g., Huang 2007; Yang 2008). Others examined the knowledge sharing between particular countries such as Mainland China and the United Kingdom (e.g., Li et al. 2014), or the links between China and Canadian universities (Hayhoe et al. 2013).

Another major cluster of themes studied was the policies, regulations and governance which covered 21 articles (22%) of the total number analyzed. Coupled with entry into the World Trade Organization, China's opening policy was seen as the driving force behind the development of cross-border higher education in China (Huang 2003; Yang 2011). Some earlier articles (M. Zhang 2009; L. Zhang 2009) examined the policy implications and challenges that were foreseen, whereas at a later stage, more studies looked into the governance issues of cross-border cooperation (Ong and Chan 2012). There are also studies that adopt a comparative approach on governance by making comparisons among different countries or regions, namely Taiwan, India, and Africa (Solomon and Wildemeersch 2006; Chan 2011; Obamba 2013). A recent article (He 2016) compared the policy orientation and reality of transnational higher

TABLE 4
Coauthorship Pattern in National Journals: By authors' affiliation

Mainland China &	Mainland China	268
	Hong Kong	1
	Canada	1
	UK	1
Hong Kong &	Hong Kong	2
Total		273

CHINESE-FOREIGN COOPERATION IN RUNNING SCHOOLS

TABLE 5
Themes of Research of Articles in International and National Journals

Themes	Number of articles (%)	
	International journals	National journals
Overview and trends	21 (22%)	246 (52.3%)
Policies, laws, regulations & governance	21 (22%)	32 (6.8%)
Students choice and experience	18 (19%)	4 (0.9%)
Institutional management	12 (13%)	48 (10.1%)
Teaching and learning	9 (9%)	55 (11.7%)
Quality assurance	7 (7%)	26 (5.5%)
Joint venture campuses	4 (4%)	3 (0.6%)
Academic profession and mobility	3 (3%)	8 (1.7%)
Cross-cultural issues		34 (7.2%)
Educational resources		14 (3.0%)
Total	95 (100%)	470 (100%)

education institutions in China. From secondary data, it claimed that it was easier to gain approval from the authorities if they collaborated with high-ranked European partners, and offered programs in IT, science, and engineering.

The third category covers the stance of the students, including their mobility, motivations, and experiences. Some research studies investigated Chinese students' motivations to study in transnational higher education in a globalized higher education market (e.g., Li and Bray 2007). It is worth noting that these articles attracted relatively high citations, as the top three most cited articles in this study all focused on student mobility and choice as shown in Appendix I (with 369, 244, and 105 citations). It could be explained by the phenomenon of massive numbers of Chinese students studying overseas. More recent empirical based research has investigated the problems or dissatisfaction experienced by students studying in Sino-foreign jointly cooperated institutes in China (e.g., Moufahim and Lim 2015). Others have argued that it is the middle class parents' choice to reproduce their class status by sending the students to these joint venture universities (Tsang 2013).

Institutional management comes fourth which focuses on the institutional and management factors that are crucial in sustaining successful cross-border partnerships. Several articles concentrated on the issues and challenges faced by the joint venture campuses in Mainland China. Academic mobility, such as the brain drain, brain gain, or circulation was identified as a specific theme which caught the attention of renowned international scholars in three articles (Rizvi 2005; Welch and Zhen 2008; Yang and Welch 2010). The citations of these articles are 81, 59, and 37, respectively.

Table 5 also shows the distribution of themes among the journal articles published by national scholars. It is interesting to discover that, overview articles composed the largest proportion, with 246 articles, taking up around 52% among all of the publications. Some authors summarized the current situation, the characteristics, the strengths, and the emerging problems of Sino-foreign cooperative education (e.g., Qin 2006). Some articles placed emphasis on the role of internationalization and globalization on the development of cross-border Chinese higher education (e.g., Xiao and Gu 2003). Other researchers focused on collaborative models and sustainability, as well as talent cultivation. In this category, 10 articles addressed the higher education cooperation between Mainland China and Hong Kong (e.g., Lin and Weng 2009), while three articles discussed the cross-strait collaboration between Mainland China and Taiwan (e.g., Mo 2013).

The second major theme concerns teaching and learning, with 55 articles, accounting for around 12% of the overall publications. Most articles in this category investigate bilingual education or English teaching in cross-border cooperation (e.g., Li and Feng 2009). The third grouping of literature focuses on institutional management and administration, occupying around 10% of the total. Some researchers focused on internal issues, such as staff management and student management (e.g., Wang 2004), while others investigated the interaction between institutions and external environments (e.g., Geng 2007), such as branding strategies, financing models, and risk management.

Topics covering law and policy, and quality assurance are also stressed. Many scholars noted that since China joined the World Trade Organization in 2001, it has become a large target in the education market for many developed countries, such as Australia, the United Kingdom, and the United States. To regulate the increasing number of Sino-foreign joint programs and institutions, China issued an important policy document in 2003, the *Regulations of the People's Republic of China on Chinese-foreign Cooperative Education*, which set down the framework for the whole endeavor.

Two other new themes have emerged which are unique in national literature, namely, cross-cultural issues and educational resources. Cross-cultural issues are aligned with many aspects of cross-border higher education, such as teaching and learning, administration and management, etc. For the national journals, much attention has been given to the following topics, such as cultural differences, educational sovereignty, core values and ideology, and political and moral education during cooperation (e.g., Meng 2008; Zha 2012). There are also several articles that discuss the theme of educational resources of high quality. National researchers stressed that import of qualified education resources is the key to success for cross-border higher education, particularly for the Chinese counterparts (e.g., Lin 2012). In addition, there are a small number of articles that focus on the experiences of teachers and students in cross-border joint programs or institutions. For the teachers, emphasis was given to the professional development of academics (e.g., Xia 2014); for the students, attention was drawn to the students' choices, satisfaction, and mobility (e.g., Zhong et al. 2012; Chen and Ho 2015).

Research Methods Analysis

The methods adopted by the researchers are shown in Table 6. After analyzing the methods of the 95 articles published in the international journals, they can be classified into two groups. Group 1 consists of 50 (or 53%) articles which are themselves divided into three subgroups. Fifteen of them provided a conceptual or theoretical framework for the themes analyzed, 18 of them provided commentary through discussions on the research topics, and 17 of them presented secondary data, either from official statistics or other sources.

The second group of journal articles (45) adopted various types of empirical based methodologies which are commonly used in the educational research field, namely case study (16), and qualitative (14) and quantitative methods (11). 3 others adopted ethnographic method, and only 1 used a mixed method. This shows that international authors have been able to use a

CHINESE-FOREIGN COOPERATION IN RUNNING SCHOOLS

TABLE 6
Methodologies of Journal Articles in International Journals

	Method	Number of articles	*Remarks*
Group 1	Conceptual	15	With theoretical framework
	Commentary	18	Discussion
	Secondary data analysis	17	Literature review, policy analysis, official data analysis
	Subtotal	50	
Group 2	Ethnographic	3	
	Case study	16	Single or multiple case studies
	Qualitative	14	Interviews, class observations
	Quantitative	11	Survey
	Mixed	1	Survey and focus group
	Sub-total	45	

Note. The classification is based on what the authors claimed in the articles as their methodologies, as well as the data presented in the articles.

wide range of methodologies in conducting the empirical research which best fits the research topics. For example, thematic clusters on overview, trends, and policies mostly draw on secondary data analysis, whereas for student-related or institutional management topics, field work including surveys, interviews, or case studies has been conducted.

Table 7 illustrates the major research methods used by national scholars. The most commonly applied method was document analysis, as 365 articles of 470 (over 77%) fall into this category. The case study method was widely adopted by national researchers with 137 articles. Figure 3 depicts the distribution of locations for the different case studies, of which Zhejiang (15), Guangdong (13), and Shanghai (13) constitute the top three. These three provinces or locations are exactly where a great deal of cross-border joint programs and institutions are situated. A small number of researchers applied the methods of survey (27) and interviews (11) to collect data. Only one researcher used ethnographic research method during the fieldwork to collect firsthand data. Another striking phenomenon is that 37 articles were largely based on commentaries and news reports, although they were included in the CSSCI.

TABLE 7
Methodologies of Journal Articles in National Journals

Method	Frequency
Documents analysis	365
Case study	137
Commentary	37
Survey	27
Interview	11
Conceptual	6
Ethnographic research	2

Note. The number is calculated by the frequency of methods that are used. One article may use multiple methods.

83

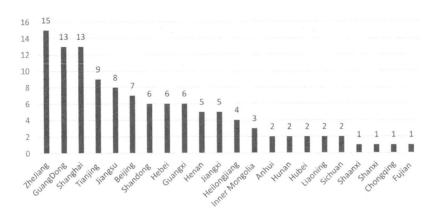

FIGURE 3 Distribution of the location of case studies, by number of articles.

Other Features

It is surprising to learn that the average length of the articles published by national scholars was around 2.5 pages. Regarding the number of references, 119 of 470 articles were without references. The average number of references for the rest of the articles was around six. Most of the references were in Chinese, and only 57 articles of 470 (12%) had references in English. For international journals, the average length per article was 17 pages, and the average number of references made per article was 36, excluding those from *International Higher Education* which are commentaries, and as such do not have references.

DISCUSSION AND CONCLUSION

Based on analysis of the findings, the implications are as follows. First, in terms of the quantity of articles, although the number of published articles in national journals is nearly five times that of international journals (470 vs. 95), there exists a big gap in their quality and their academic rigor. Another obvious difference is the length of the articles. Those published in international journals have an average page length of 17, except those that appeared in *International Higher Education*, which mainly contain commentaries instead of research papers. On the other hand, the average length of articles published in national journals is merely 2.5 pages, and 119 of 470 articles are without references.

Another yardstick by which to evaluate the quality of the articles is their impact in academia based on the citation records. Appendix 1 shows the articles which have attracted over 50 citations in Google Scholars. Among the highly cited articles, the most common theme covers student mobility and the brain drain: Altbach (2004; 369 citations), Li and Bray (2007; 244 citations), Bodycott (2009; 105 citations), Rizvi (2005; 81 citations), and Welch and Zhen (2008; 59 citations). Moreover, although as shown in the previous section, more authors from Mainland China contribute to the articles, most cited ones go to Western scholars. Hong Kong also has substantial representation. It is worth noting that among these authors, some are Chinese nationals affiliated to foreign institutions.

CHINESE-FOREIGN COOPERATION IN RUNNING SCHOOLS

Third, the engagement of current national researchers in the international academic community is inadequate. For example, of 273 coauthored articles in national literature, 268 (98%) articles were coauthored among researchers from Mainland China. Only three articles were collaborative publications by authors affiliated with institutions between Mainland China and other countries or regions. This factor might be attributed to a language barrier. Another indicator is that among national literature, only 57 (12%) of 470 articles have references in English, and the rest of national articles solely cite Chinese literature. This observation echoes similar findings by Jung (2015), Chen and Hu (2012), and Arimoto (2000) that the higher education community in Korea, China, and Japan needs to employ a more open and outward-looking view in their research.

Fourth, in terms of the specific themes, general analyses on overviews, trends and policy issues has dominated the current literature in both the international and national journals. For instance, in the national journals, the numbers of overview analyses account for more than 50% of the whole literature. The writing styles and genres are more akin to government working reports commenting on current situations and providing suggestions. For the international journals, articles discussing overall trends (22%) and policy issues (22%) take up 44% in total. In terms of methodologies, international authors have adopted various types of research methods as driven by the thematic topics. However, only half of the current literature is empirically based research. In national literature, the method of document analysis is heavily used, and a large proportion of national research is a combination of partial literature reviews and personal experiences, lacking qualified firsthand data and rigorous analysis.

Finally, microlevel analysis, such as the students and teachers as a research focus, is seriously under-researched both in international journals and national journals. For students, over 1.5 million Chinese college students graduated from these joint programs or institutes, and yet in national journals only 4 articles (0.8%) of the 470 articles put students under the spotlight. On the other hand, in international journals, 18 articles (19%) focus on student choices, motivations, and experiences. In the context of Mainland China, the lives and experiences of students in cross-border joint programs or institutions are severely underresearched. This is most likely due to the fact that this type of research requires researchers to commit to a relatively long duration of field work, which would be difficult for both national and international scholars. Nevertheless, it would be worthwhile to have more empirical studies on students' experiences, as well as their employability compared to the massive numbers of graduates from main stream colleges. Regarding the life experiences of teachers, only three articles (3%) in international journals and eight articles (1.7%) in national journals put them forward as the focus of analysis.

To conclude, the existing literature on cross-border Chinese higher education could be viewed as an emerging field in its infancy, particularly in terms of theoretical maturity and methodological sophistication. Much academic effort is required for the growth of the field, particularly in the following aspects. First, more collaboration between Chinese scholars and international scholars is needed to address the various topics within cross-border Chinese higher education. In particular, for Chinese scholars, more engagement with the international community would enhance the dialogue and pave the way for new opportunities in further research.

Second, more studies at the microlevel, in particular the life experiences and career paths of students who are enrolled in cross-border joint programs and institutions deserve further investigation. For instance, who chose this new model of education for them? What are the links,

CHINESE-FOREIGN COOPERATION IN RUNNING SCHOOLS

if any, among the social class, family choices, educational strategies, and capital accumulation? What are the roles of cross-border higher education in social mobility and social reproduction, if any? What are the implications for social equality and social justice in Chinese society?

Third, more diversified and rigorous research methods are suggested so as to collect and analyze qualified first-hand data. Research papers which solely rely on second-hand data are not adequate or convincing enough to address and explain the complexities of topics in the collaboration of cross-border higher education. For example, more critical analysis needs to be conducted through data collection from longitudinal or mixed research methods, which may, in turn, result in more significant findings, meaningful results, and deeper impacts.

Fourth, from the perspective of policy orientation, the primary objective of the Chinese central government to encourage Chinese-foreign higher education collaboration is to enhance the quality and capacity of the higher education system in China. Since its implementation over the past decade, to what extent have the policy goals been achieved, and how and why are there any gaps between the policy intention and reality? Despite these seemingly obvious questions, all of the above thematic topics on policy have caught minimal attention from national scholars.

Fifth, more research can be conducted at an institutional and program level. There is paucity of in-depth empirical research regarding what has taken place at the institutional and program level, although over 577 universities or colleges have engaged in joint programs and institutions in China over the years. As insiders, national researchers may have an advantage in conducting institutional level research.

Finally, the complex interactions among local, national, and global stakeholders in cross-border cooperation is worth further attention and deeper analysis. In the discourse of the existing national research, cross-border cooperation is usually uncritically viewed as an inevitable trend or an essential part of internationalization without analyzing the unintended consequences of educational marketization and unequal power relations in the collaboration process. In addition, among the national scholars, the dimension of internationalization and globalization is overwhelmingly stressed, while the localization and indigenization of knowledge and institutions are surprisingly neglected.

In the current study we adopted a bibliometric approach to provide quantitative analysis on cross-border Chinese higher education in national and international literature. Ninety-five articles in international journals and 470 articles in national journals were collected and analyzed. It provides an overview of how the field has developed over the past two decades, as well as offering a comparison between the authorship patterns, thematic clusters and research methods undertaken by both national and international scholars. One limitation is that the selection is only confined to journal articles published during the period. For further studies, it is suggested that a qualitative approach with content analysis of the particular themes is developed so as to tap into the theoretical orientations of the researchers. Other types of publications could also be included to extend the breadth of the corpus.

NOTES

1. International journals included, for example, *Journal of Studies in International Education* (13), *International Higher Education* (12), *Frontiers of Education in China* (11), *Chinese Education & Society* (9), *Higher Education* (6), *Asia Pacific Journal of Education* (4), *Higher Education Policy* (4), *Globalization, Societies and Education* (2), and others.

CHINESE-FOREIGN COOPERATION IN RUNNING SCHOOLS

2. National journals included, for example, *Education and Vocation* (39), *China Adult Education* (36), *China Higher Education* (23), *Research in Education Development* (22), *Heilongjiang Researches on Higher Education* (19), *Jiangsu Higher Education* (19), *Education Exploration* (16), *Education Research* (15), *China Higher Education Research* (15), *Higher Education Exploration* (13), *Research in Higher Education of Engineering* (12), *Chinese Vocational and Technical Education* (11), *Theory and Practice of Education* (10), *Modern Education Management* (10), and others.

REFERENCES

Altbach, P. 2004. Higher education crosses borders: Can the United States remain the top destination for foreign students? *Change* 36 (2):18–25.

Arimoto, A. 2000. Recent developments of higher education research and higher education policy in Japan. In *The institutional basis of higher education research: Experiences and perspectives*, eds. I. S. Schwarz and U. Teichler 93–106. Dordrecht: Kluwer Academic Publishers.

Bodycott, P. 2009. Choosing a higher education study abroad destination: What mainland Chinese parents and students rate as important. *Journal of Research in International Education* 8:349–373.

Chan, S. J. 2011. Cross-border educational collaboration between Taiwan and China: The implications for educational governance. *Asia Pacific Journal of Higher Education* 31:311–23.

Chen, L. Y., and S. C. Ho. 2015. Student choice of Chinese-foreign cooperative university in Mainland China from the perspective of information strategies. *Fudan Education Forum* 13 (3):71–7.

Chen, S., and L. Hu. 2012. Higher education research as a field in China: Its formation and current landscape. *Higher Education Research and Development* 31 (5):655–66. doi:10.1080/07294360.2012.692116

Chinese State Council. 2003. *Regulations of the People's Republic of China on Chinese-Foreign Cooperation in Running Schools.* http://www.moe.edu.cn/publicfiles/business/htmlfiles/moe/moe_861/200506/8646.html

Geng, D. L. 2007. Stakeholder analysis for Sino-foreign cooperative education. (in Chinese). *Higher Education Exploration* 1:59–63.

Hayhoe, R., J. Pan, and Q. Zha. 2013. Lessons from the legacy of Canada-China university linkages. *Frontiers of Education in China* 8:80–104.

He, L. 2016. Transnational higher education institutions in China: A comparison of policy orientation and reality. *Journal of Studies in International Education* 20 (1):79–95. doi:10.1177/1028315315602931

Huang, F. 2003. Policy and practice of the internationalization of higher education in China. *Journal of Studies in International Education* 7:225–40.

Huang, F. 2007. Internationalization of higher education in the developing and emerging countries: A focus on transnational higher education in Asia. *Journal of Studies in International Education* 11 (3–4):421–32. doi:10.1177/1028315307303919

Jung, J. 2015. Higher education research as a field of study in South Korea: Inward but starting to look outward. *Higher Education Policy* 28:495–515. doi:10.1057/hep.2015.18

Knight, J. 2007. Cross-border tertiary education: An introduction. In *Cross-border tertiary education: A way toward capacity development*. Geneva, Switzerland: OECD and World Bank.

Kosmützky, A., and R. Putty. 2016. Transcending borders and traversing boundaries: A systematic review of the literature on transnational, offshore, cross-border, and borderless higher education. *Journal of Studies in International Education* 20 (1):8–33. doi:10.1177/1028315315604719

Li, G. S., and C. Y. Feng. 2009. Bilingual teaching model in Sino-foreign joint programs. (in Chinese). *Journal of Higher Education* 30 (1):79–83.

Li, M., and M. Bray. 2007. Cross-border flows of students for higher education: Push-pull factors and motivations of mainland Chinese students. *Higher Education* 53:791–818. doi:10.1007/s10734-005-5423-3

Li, X., J. Roberts, Y. Yan, and H. Tan. 2014. Knowledge sharing in China–UK higher education alliances. *International Business Review* 23:343–55. doi:10.1016/j.ibusrev.2013.05.001

Li, X. H., and F. Y. Jiang. 2007. Research on transnational higher education in the West: Conceptions and issues. *Peking University Education Review* 5:120–27.

Lin, J. H. 2012. Import of high quality education resources in Sino-foreign cooperative education. (in Chinese). *Educational Research* 10:34–38.

Lin, J. H., and H. X. Weng. 2009. Higher education cooperation between Mainland China and Hong Kong: Histories and trends. (in Chinese). *China Higher Education Research* 6:51–4.

Meng, Z. Y. 2008. Cultural conflicts in Sino-foreign cooperative education. (in Chinese). *China Higher Education Research* 11:72–74.

Ministry of Education. 2013. Chinese-Foreign Cooperation in Running Schools. http://www.crs.jsj.edu.cn/index.php/default/news/index/80 (accessed March 20, 2016).

Mo, Y. W. 2013. Vocational education cooperation between Fujian and Taiwan: Status quo, problems and policy implications. (in Chinese). *Education and Vocation* 33:15–7.

Moufahim, M., and M. Lim. 2015. The other voices of international higher education: An empirical study of students' perceptions of British university education in China. *Globalisation, Societies and Education* 13:437–54. doi:10.1080/14767724.2014.959476

Obamba, M. 2013. The Dragon's deal: Sino-African cooperation in higher education. *International Higher Education* 72.

Ong, L. C., and K. K. Chan. 2012. Transnational higher education and challenges for university governance in China. *Higher Education Policy* 25:151–70.

Qin, M. Q. 2006. Sino-foreign joint school operation: Status quo and policy implications. (in Chinese). *Higher Education Research* 5:34–9.

Rizvi, F. 2005. Rethinking "brain drain" in the era of globalisation. *Asia Pacific Journal of Education* 25 (2):175–92. doi:10.1080/02188790500337965

Solomon, D. A., and D. Wildemeersch. 2006. Dealing with cross-border higher education: Comparing the Chinese and the Indian ways. *Tertium Comparationis* 12:145–163.

Tao, L., and J. L. Shen. 2006. Literature review on international cooperation in running schools in China. *Education of Chinese Medicine* 25 (4):5–10.

Tsang, E. 2013. The quest for higher education by the Chinese middle class: Retrenching social mobility? *Higher Education* 66:653–68. doi:10.1007/s10734-013-9627-7

Wang, L. 2012. Quantitative analysis on the domestic study of Sino-foreign cooperation in running schools (1995-2010). *Modern Education Management* 4:14–8.

Wang, M. L. 2004. Overseas staff management in Sino-foreign joint programs. (in Chinese). *Heilongjiang Researches on Higher Education* 9:48–50.

Welch, A. R., and Zhen, Z. 2008. Higher education and global talent flows: Brain drain, overseas Chinese intellectuals, and diasporic knowledge. *Higher Education Policy* 21:519–37. doi:10.1057/hep.2008.20

Xia, B. B. 2014. Teachers' professional development in Sino-foreign cooperative education. (in Chinese). *Journal of National Academy of Education Administration* 12:68–72.

Xiao, G. X., and G. H. Gu. 2003. Globalization and Sino-foreign cooperation in running schools. (in Chinese). *Heilongjiang Researches on Higher Education* 5:9–12.

Yang, R. 2008. Transnational higher education in China: Contexts, characteristics and concerns. *Australian Journal of Education* 52 (3): 272–86. doi:10.1177/000494410805200305

Yang, R. 2011. China's entry into the WTO and higher education. *International Higher Education* 24.

Yang, R., and A. R. Welch. 2010. Globalisation, transnational academic mobility and the Chinese knowledge diaspora: An Australian case study. *Discourse (Abingdon)* 31:593–607. doi:10.1080/01596306.2010.516940

Zha, Q. 2012. Transnational higher education in China: Toward a critical culturalist research agenda. *University Education Science* 2:12–9.

Zhang, L. 2009. Policy direction and development trends for Sino-foreign partnership schools. Chinese Education & Society 42 (4):11–22.

Zhang, M. 2009. New era, new policy: Cross-border education and Sino-foreign cooperation in running schools in the eyes of a fence-sitter. Chinese Education & Society 42 (4):23–40.

Zhong, B. L., H. T. Zhou, and H. H. Xia. 2012. Students' satisfaction on cross-border joint-programs and institutions. *China Higher Education Research* 9:22–6.

APPENDIX

Appendix 1
Articles With More Than 50 Citations in Google Scholars

Journal Articles	Authors, Year published	Number of citations
Higher education crosses borders: Can the United States remain the top destination for foreign students?	Philip Altbach (2004)	369
Cross-border flows of students for higher education: Push-pull factors and motivations of mainland Chinese students	Li Mei & Mark Bray (2007)	244
Choosing a higher education study abroad destination: What mainland Chinese parents and students rate as important	Peter Bodycott (2009)	105
Internationalization of higher education in the developing and emerging countries: A focus on transnational higher education in Asia	Huang Futao (2007)	105
Policy and practice of the internationalization of higher education in China	Huang Futao (2003)	87
Rethinking "brain drain" in the era of globalisation	Fazal Rizvi (2005)	81
Don't leave me hanging on the Anglophone: The potential for online distance higher education in the Asia-Pacific	Simon Marginson (2004)	69
The growing importance of the privateness in education: Challenges for higher education governance in China	Mok KH (2009)	64
Higher education and global talent flows: Brain drain, overseas Chinese intellectuals, and diasporic knowledge	Anthony Welch & Zhang Zhen (2008)	59
The development of transnational higher education in China: A comparative study of research universities and teaching universities	Fang Wenhong (2012)	59
Cultural differences, learning styles and transnational education	Troy Heffernan, Mark Morrison, Parikshit Basu & Arthur Sweeney (2012)	56

Note. The citation data mentioned in Appendix 1, to the best of our belief, were accurate as of 28 February 2016. Omissions of author(s) or works are wholly unintentional.

CHINESE-FOREIGN COOPERATION IN RUNNING SCHOOLS

Appendix 2
List of International Journals by Thematic Clusters

Authors/Articles	Number of citations
Overview and trends	
1. Huang, F. (2007). Internationalization of higher education in the developing and emerging countries: A focus on transnational higher education in Asia. *Journal of Studies in International Education*, 11(3-/4), 421–432.	105
2. Yang, R. (2008). Transnational higher education in China: Contexts, characteristics and concerns. *Australian Journal of Education*, 52(3), 272–286. 2. Yang, R. (2008). Transnational higher education in China: Contexts, characteristics and concerns. *Australian Journal of Education*, 52(3), 272–286.	42
3. Gu Jianxin (2009). Transnational education: Current developments and policy implications. *Frontiers of Education in China*, 4(4), 624–649.	25
4. Li, Xiaoqing, Roberts, Joanne, Yan, Yanni & Tan, Hui (2014). Knowledge sharing in China-UK higher education alliances. *International Business Review*, 23(2), 343–355.	15
5. Li, Xiaoqing & Roberts, Joanne (2012). A stages approach to the internationalization of higher education? The entry of UK universities into China. *The Service Industries Journal*, 32(7), 1011–1038.	14
6. Hayhoe, R., Pan Julia & Zha Qiang (2013). Lessons from the legacy of Canada-China university linkages. *Frontiers of Education in China*, 8(1), 80–104.	12
7. Chiang, Li-Chuan (2012). Trading on the West's strength: The dilemmas of transnational higher education in East Asia. *Higher Education Policy*, 25(2), 171–189.	12
8. Altbach, P. & Postiglione, G.A (2012). Hong Kong's academic advantage. *International Higher Education*, 66 Winter. 8. Altbach, P. & Postiglione, G.A (2012). Hong Kong's academic advantage. *International Higher Education*, 66 Winter.	8
9. Hou Junxia, Montgomery Catherine & McDowell Liz (2014). Exploring the diverse motivations of transnational higher education in China: Complexities and contradictions. *Journal of Education for Teaching*, 40(3), 300–318.	6
10. Postiglione, G.A. (2011). Expansion, consolidation, and globalization. *International Higher Education*, 24 Summer. 10. Postiglione, G.A. (2011). Expansion, consolidation, and globalization. *International Higher Education*, 24 Summer.	6
11. Qin Meiqiong (2007). The current situations of Chinese-foreign cooperation in operating schools and its countermeasures. *Frontiers of Education in China*, July, 2(3), 336–348.	5
12. Yang, R. (2014). China's strategy for the internationalization of higher education: An overview. *Frontiers of Education in China*, 9(2), 151–162.	4
13. Welch, A. (2012). China-ASEAN relations in higher education: An analytical framework. *Frontiers of Education in China*, 7(4), 465–485.	4
14. Welch, A. (2007). The minnow and the whale: Singapore-China relations in higher education. *International Higher Education*, 46 Winter.	4
15. Gu Ling (2006). On the cultural legacy of the Cold War: Sino-US educational exchange (1949 – 1990). *Frontiers of Education in China*, 1(4), 487–504.	4
16. Dow, Ewan G. (2010). Look before you leap: Underestimating Chinese student history, Chinese university setting and Chinese university steering in Sino-British higher education joint ventures? *Globalisation, Societies and Education*, 8(4), 497–526.	2
17. Lin, Jinhui & Liu, Zhiping (2009). New exploration in the development strategy of "going out" for Chinese-foreign cooperation in higher education. *Chinese Education & Society*, July - August, 42(4), 78–87.	1
18. Welch, A. (2015). A new epistemic silk road? The Chinese knowledge diaspora, and its implications for the Europe of knowledge. *European Review*, 23, S95–S111.	1

(Continued)

CHINESE-FOREIGN COOPERATION IN RUNNING SCHOOLS

Appendix 2
Continued

Authors/Articles	Number of citations
19. Ringwald, K. (2008). Transferring management knowledge in Anglo-Chinese higher education collaboration: Are we speaking the same language? *Industry and Higher Education*, 22(5), 315–326.	NA
20. Guidoin, R., Wang Lu & Douville Yvan (2015). Towards mutuality in the Canada-China relationship: The experience of the department of surgery at Laval University since the 1980s. *Frontiers of Education in China*, 10(3), 384–400.	NA
21. Hayhoe, R., Marginson, S., Yuzhuo, Cai, Yuzhuo & Jiang, Kai (2014). Responses to Yang Rui's "China's strategy for internationalization of higher education: An overview". *Frontiers of Education in China*, 9(2), 163–187.	NA
Policies, regulations & governance	
1. Huang, F. (2003). Policy and practice of the internationalization of higher education in China. *Journal of Studies in International Education*, September, 7(3), 225–240.	87
2. Mok, K.H. (2009). The growing importance of the privateness in education: Challenges for higher education governance in China. *Compare: A Journal of Comparative and International Education*, 39(1), 35–49.	64
3. Yang, R. (2011). China's entry into the WTO and higher education. *International Higher Education*, 24 Summer.	12
4. Altbach, P. (2006). Chinese higher education in an Open-door era. *International Higher Education*, 45 Fall.	12
5. Chan, Sheng-Ju (2011). Cross-border educational collaboration between Taiwan and China: The implications for educational governance. *Asia Pacific Journal of Higher Education*, 31(3) 311–323.	7
6. Pinna, Cristina (2009). EU-China relations in higher education. *Asia Europe Journal*, 7(3–4) 505–527.	7
7. Yang, R. (2011). International organizations, changing governance and China's policy making in higher education: An analysis of the World Bank and the World Trade Organization. *Asia Pacific Journal of Education* 30(4) 419–431.	6
8. Pan, Maoyuan (2009). An analytical differentiation of the relationship between education sovereignty and education rights. *Chinese Education & Society*, July–August, 42(4), 88–96.	6
9. Ong Lok Chung & Chan, KK David (2012). Transnational higher education and challenges for university governance in China. *Higher Education Policy*, 25, 151–170.	5
10. Solomon, A. D. & Wildemeersch, D. (2006). Dealing with cross-border higher education: Comparing the Chinese and the Indian ways. *Tertium Comparationis*, 12(2), 145–163.	5
11. Yang, R. (2012). Internationalization, regionalization, and soft power: China's relations with ASEAN member countries in higher education. *Frontiers of Education in China*, 7(4), 486–507.	5
12. Obamba, M. (2013). The Dragon's deal: Sino-African cooperation in higher education. *International Higher Education*, 72 Summer.	3
13. Postiglione, G.A. (2015). Research universities for national rejuvenation and global influence: China's search for a balanced model. *Higher Education*, 70: 235–250.	2
14. Xu, Xiaozhou & Kan, Yue (2013). Cross-border higher education in China in the globalized world: The perspective of the World Trade Organization's general agreement on trade in services. *KEDI Journal of Educational Policy*, 10(2), 199–220.	2
15. Zhang, Minxuan (2009). New era, new policy: Cross-border education and Sino-foreign cooperation in running schools in the eyes of a fence-sitter. *Chinese Education & Society*, 42(4), 23–40.	1

(Continued)

CHINESE-FOREIGN COOPERATION IN RUNNING SCHOOLS

Appendix 2
Continued

Authors/Articles	Number of citations
16. Zhang, Li (2009). Policy direction and development trends for Sino-foreign partnership schools. *Chinese Education & Society*, July - August, 42(4), 11–22.	1
17. Zhou, Mansheng (2009). Education imports and exports in the framework of the World Trade Organization and adjustments of education legislation and policy making in China. *Chinese Education & Society*, July – August, 42(4), 41–53.	1
18. Garrett, R. (2004). China: Regulation and scale of foreign activity. *International Higher Education*, 34 Winter.	1
19. He, Lan (2016). Transnational higher education institutions in China: A comparison of policy orientation and reality. *Journal of Studies in International Education*, 20(1). 79–95	NA
20. Lan, Jun (2012). Feasibility analysis of developing cross-border network education in China. *Physics Procedia*, 33, 1979–1985.	NA
21. Qin, Meiqiong (2009). Analysis of the status quo and suggested policy adjustments for Sino-foreign cooperation in running schools. *Chinese Education & Society*, 42(4), 54–67.	NA
Students choice and experiences	
1. Altbach, P. (2004). Higher education crosses borders: Can the United States remain the top destination for foreign students? *Change*, 36(2), 18–25.	369
2. Li, M. & Bray, M. (2007). Cross-border flows of students for higher education: Push-pull factors and motivations of mainland Chinese students. *Higher Education*, 53(6), 791–818.	244
3. Bodycott, P. (2009). Choosing a higher education study abroad destination: What mainland Chinese parents and students rate as important. *Journal of Research in International Education*, 8 (3), 349–373.	105
4. Bodycott, P. & Lai, A. (2012). Influence and implications of Chinese culture in the decision to undertake cross-border higher education. *Journal of Studies in International Education*, 16, 252–270.	33
5. Mok, K.H. & Xu, Xiaozhou (2008). When China opens to the world: A study of transnational higher education in Zhejiang, China. *Asia Pacific Education Review*, 9(4) 393–408.	22
6. Li, M. & Bray, M. (2007). Social class and cross-border higher education: Mainland Chinese students in Hong Kong and Macau. *Journal of International Migration and Integration*, 7(4), 407–424.	20
7. Pan, Su-Yan (2008). Changes and challenges in the flow of international human capital: China's experience. *Journal of Studies in International Education*, 14(3), 259–288.	19
8. Fang, Wenhong & Wang Shen (2014). Chinese students' choice of transnational higher education in a globalized higher education market: A case study of W university. *Journal of Studies in International Education*, 18(5), 475–494.	8
9. Tsang, E. (2013). The quest for higher education by the Chinese middle class: Retrenching social mobility? *Higher Education*, 66(6), 653–668.	6
10. To, W.M.. Lung, Jane W.Y., Lai, Linda S.L. & Lai, T.M. (2014). Destination choice of cross-border Chinese students: An importance-performance analysis. *Educational Studies*, 40(1), 63–80. 10.	4
11. Cao, Ling & Ly Thi Tran (2015). Pathway from vocational education and associate degree to higher education: Chinese international students in Australia. *Asia Pacific Journal of Education*, 35(2), 274–289.	4
12. Xu, Cora Lingling (2015). Identity and cross-border student mobility: The mainland China-Hong Kong experience. *European Education Research Journal*, 14(1) 65–73.	3
13. Hou, Junxia & McDowell Liz (2014). Learning together? Experiences on a China–U.K. articulation program in Engineering. *Journal of Studies in International Education*, 18(3) 223–240.	2

(Continued)

CHINESE-FOREIGN COOPERATION IN RUNNING SCHOOLS

Appendix 2
Continued

Authors/Articles	Number of citations
14. Ghazarian, P.G. (2014). Changing destinations: Ideal attraction and actual movement of cross-border tertiary students from mainland China. *International Education Journal*, 13 (1), 1–16.	2
15. Moufahim, M. & Lim, M. (2015). The other voices of international higher education: An empirical study of students' perceptions of British university education in China. *Globalisation, Societies and Education*, 13(4), 437–454.	NA
16. Hohner, M. & Panagiotis Tsigaris (2012). Students' perception of quality for a business program delivered in Canada and China. *Journal of International Education in Business*, 5(1), 37–49.	NA
17. Fang, W., Clarke, A. & Wei, Y. (2015). Empty success or brilliant failure: An analysis of Chinese students' study abroad experience in a collaborative Master of Education program. *Journal of Studies in International Education*, 1–24.	NA
18. Zha, Qiang (2012). Study abroad fever among Chinese students. *International Higher Education*, 69 Fall.	NA
Institutional management	
1. Fang Wenhong (2012). The development of transnational higher education in China: A comparative study of research universities and teaching universities. *Journal of Studies in International Education*, 16(1), 5–23.	59
2. Ennew, Christine T. & Yang Fujia (2009). Foreign universities in China: A case study. *European Journal of Education*, 44(1), 25–36	33
3. Feng, Y. (2013). University of Nottingham Ningbo China and Xi'an Jiaotong-Liverpool University: Globalization of higher education in China. *Higher Education*, 65(4), 471–485.	16
4. Willis, M. (2004). The application of the Chinese sense of "balance" to agreements signed between Chinese and foreign institutions in the Chinese higher education sector: Adding depth to a popular cultural concept. *Journal of Marketing for Higher Education*, 14(1), 107–121.	9
5. Jie, Yiyun (2010). International partnerships: A game theory perspective. *New Directions for Higher Education*, 150, 43–54 Sum.	8
6. Healey, N, M. (2006). The challenges of leading an international branch campus: The "lived experience" of in-country senior managers. *Journal of Studies in International Education*, 20(1), 61–78.	3
7. Li, Xiaoqing; Roberts, Joanne; Yan, Yanni & Tan, Hui (2016). Management of cultural differences under various forms of China–UK higher education strategic alliances. *Studies in Higher Education*. 41(04), 774–798.	1
8. Chan Sheng-ju & Chang Fang-Min (2013). Sharing the emerging educational market in China: Cross-border EMBA programmes in China, Hong Kong, and Taiwan. *Asian Education and Development Studies*, 2(2), 112–126.	1
9. Li, Aisi (2014). Towards building direct educational partnership: The foundation of Shanxi University in 1902. *Frontiers of Education in China*, 9(2), 188–210.	NA
10. Wei, Shuguang & Liu, Xianjun (2015). Institutionalized mutuality in Canada-China management education collaboration. *Frontiers of Education in China*, 10(3), 356–383.	NA
11. Liu, Huacong & Metcalfe, A.S. (2016). Internationalizing Chinese higher education: A glonacal analysis of local layers and conditions. *Higher Education*, 71, 399–413.	NA
12. Cai Li & Hall Christine (2015). Motivations, expectations, and experiences of expatriate academic staff on an international branch campus in China. *Journal of Studies in International Education*, 20.	NA

(Continued)

CHINESE-FOREIGN COOPERATION IN RUNNING SCHOOLS

Appendix 2
Continued

Authors/Articles	Number of citations
Teaching and Learning	
1. Marginson, S. (2004). Don't leave me hanging on the Anglophone: The potential for online distance higher education in the Asia-Pacific region. *Higher Education Quarterly*, 2004, 58(2–3), 74–113.	69
2. Heffernan, T., Morrison, M., Basu, P. & Sweeney, A. (2010). Cultural differences, learning styles and transnational education. *Journal of Higher Education Policy and Management*, 32(1), 27–39.	56
3. Debowski, S. (2005). Across the divide: Teaching a transnational MBA in a second language. *Higher Education Research and Development*, 24(3), 265–280.	22
4. Wilkins, S. & Urbanovi⊠, J. (2014). English as the lingua franca in transnational higher education: Motives and prospects of institutions that teach in languages other than English. *Journal of Studies in International Education*, 18(5), 405–425.	9
5. Kuroda, C (2014). The new sphere of international student education in Chinese higher education. *Journal of Studies in International Education*, 18(5), 45–462.	7
6. Carolan, L. & Wang, Lijuan (2012). Reflections on a transnational peer review of teaching. *ELT Journal*, 66(1), 71–80.	6
7. Pullman, A. (2015). Racialized bodies, pliable minds: Ethnography on the fringe of transnational education. *Asia Pacific Journal of Education*, 35(1), 1–13.	1
8. Scott, J.D. (2014). Memoir as a form of auto-ethnographic research for exploring the practice of transnational higher education in China. *Higher Education Research & Development*, 33(4), 757–768.	NA
9. Wang Songliang, Caldwell, C., Wei, Liqing & Su, Haiyan (2015). Ten years Chinese-Canadian collaboration in undergraduate education in Fujian Agriculture and Forestry University of China: Curriculum development. *Frontiers of Education in China*, 10(3), 427–438.	NA
Quality Assurance	
1. Pyvis, D. (2011). The need for context-sensitive measures of educational quality in transnational higher education. *Teaching in Higher Education*, 16(6), 733–744.	22
2. Tan, Z. (2009). Internationalization of higher education in China: Chinese-foreign cooperation in running schools and the introduction of high-quality foreign educational resources. *International Education Studies*, 2(3), 166–171.	11
3. Zhou, Chaocheng (2009). Analysis of three frameworks for quality assurance in Sino-foreign cooperation for running schools. *Chinese Education & Society*, July–August, 42(4), 87–107.	2
4. Wulf, C. & Takhar, J. (2009). Asia vs. the 'others': How to bridge the intercultural gap in cross-border higher education. *International Journal of Management in Education*. 3–4, 375–387.	1
5. Lin, Jinhui & Liu, Zhiping (2009). Appropriate importation and effective utilization of top quality foreign higher education resources for Sino-foreign cooperation in running schools. *Chinese Education & Society*, July–August, 42(4), 68–77.	1
6. Ma, Wanhua & Yue Yun (2015). Internationalization for quality in Chinese research universities: Student perspectives. *Higher Education*, 70, 217–234.	1
7. Li, Yadong & Jiang Yanqiao (2009). The need for context-sensitive measures of educational quality in transnational higher education. *Chinese Education & Society*, 42(4), 108–118.	NA
Joint venture campuses	
1. Ozturgut, O (2008). Joint venture campuses in China. *International Higher Education*, 53 Fall.	1
2. Stanfield, D. & Wang Qi (2012). Full scale branch campuses in China. *International Higher Education*, 69 Fall.	NA
3. Hayhoe, R. & Pan, J. (2015). Joint-venture universities in China: Shanghai and Shenzhen comparisons. *International Higher Education*, 81 Summer.	NA
4. Helms, R. (2008). Transnational education in China. *International Higher Education*, 53 Fall.	NA

(*Continued*)

CHINESE-FOREIGN COOPERATION IN RUNNING SCHOOLS

Appendix 2
Continued

Authors/Articles	Number of citations
Academic profession and mobility	
1. Fazal Rizvi (2005). Rethinking "brain drain" in the era of globalisation. *Asia Pacific Journal of Education*, 25(2), 175–192.	82
2. Welch, A. & Zhang Zhen (2008). Higher education and global talent flows: Brain drain, overseas Chinese intellectuals, and diasporic knowledge. *Higher Education Policy*, 21, 519–537.	59
3. Yang, R. & Welch, A. (2010). Globalisation, transnational academic mobility and the Chinese knowledge diaspora: An Australian case study. *Discourse (Abingdon): studies in the cultural politics of education*, 31(5), 593–607.	37

Independent Chinese-Foreign Collaborative Universities and their Quest for Legitimacy

Li Zhang and Kevin Kinser

Abstract: A new organization often encounters the liability of newness that increases its chance of failing as a startup enterprise (Freeman, Carroll, and Hannan 1983). New organizations located in a foreign country also face the liability of foreignness (Zaheer and Mosakowski 1997), as cultural differences make new foreign ventures especially risky. Moreover, according to organizational theory, legitimacy is critical to an organization's success or failure (Meyer and Rowan 1977; Singh, Tucker, and House 1986; Vanhonackers 2000; Bianchi and Ostale 2006; Diez-Martin, Prado-Roman, and Blanco-González 2013). By gaining legitimacy, organizations can obtain the resources they need to become sustainable. Similarly, a lack of legitimacy can lead an organization to lose (or never establish) its social support, thus increasing its chance of failure.

The liabilities of newness and foreignness aptly describe the independent Chinese-foreign universities that have been set up in China. They risk failure if they are not able to navigate the foreign system and regulative environment as a new and novel organizational form. In addition, they have to confront the challenge of establishing legitimacy in order to survive and develop.

The University of Nottingham Ningbo, Xi'an Jiaotong Liverpool University, and New York University Shanghai are three universities representing different stages of development as Chinese-foreign universities. We discuss how these institutions are confronting the twin liabilities of newness and foreignness, and how they are developing legitimacy in China. We use Scott's (1995) institutional pillars and Suchman's legitimacy framework to describe and analyze the strategies these institutions use to gain legitimacy in China. Forty-two interviews were conducted with presidents, vice presidents, senior administrators, faculty, parents and students, and employers about these three international universities (IUs). In addition, experts on Chinese-Foreign Collaboration in Running Schools (CCRS) and government officials were also interviewed to have a thorough understanding of the legitimacy issues with these institutions. We conclude with implications for the policy and practice of Chinese-foreign collaborations in higher education.

INTRODUCTION

Cross-border higher education has received much attention from researchers during the past decade, including research on student mobility, program mobility and institutional mobility. In particular, institutional mobility has emerged to become a key feature of cross-border education. In China, institutional mobility occurs within an official framework referred to as CCRS. The name conveys the important fact that, under regulations issued by Ministry of Education, each cross-border activity in China is a partnership between a Chinese institution and a foreign education provider.

China is the second largest importer of international branch campuses in the world, after the UAE, with 28 Chinese-foreign campuses already in existence (Cross-Border Education Research Team 2015). However, in the China context, these institutions are not really branch campuses of foreign institutions; they are referred to as IUs or international colleges. IUs are those Chinese-foreign institutions with legal person status,[1] while the international colleges are Chinese-foreign institutions without legal person status. Currently, there are nine IUs and 47 international colleges (Ministry of Education 2015).[2]

Scholars have conducted research in CCRS from multiple aspects, including but not limited to the importance and functions of CCRS, partnership models, marketing and promotion of CCRS, moral education and student management, development of foreign faculty, tuition, quality assurance, education sovereignty, and unique case studies (Tao and Shen 2006; Cheng and Cheng 2007). However, very few of these research articles are empirical studies. To date, the study of legitimacy of these international institutions in China is absent, not only because legitimacy is a very elusive and complex concept, but also legitimacy is an understudied subject with higher education institutions worldwide. Our research can fill these gaps by focusing on the legitimacy of CCRS in China, with specific attention to the Chinese IUs.

Existing research from organizational studies indicates that the establishment and maintenance of legitimacy is one of the critical issues multinational enterprises face when they enter foreign markets (Kostova and Zaheer 1999). Setting up branch campuses on foreign soil is a high-risk development strategy (Becker 2009; Borgos 2013), which similarly face the challenge of establishing and maintaining legitimacy (Farrugia and Lane 2013; Lane, Kinser, and Knox 2013; Borgos 2013). The IUs in China are a new form of higher education, which lacks both traditional social standing and a significant track record. When organizations are established in a new locale, they face the liability of newness (Freeman, Carroll, and Hannan 1983); new organizations located on foreign soil also face liability of foreignness (Zaheer and Mosakowski 1997). The liabilities of newness and foreignness apply within the higher education sector when institutions develop campuses abroad. By gaining legitimacy, the enterprises can acquire the resources and the market acceptance they need for their survival and prosperity (Dowling and Pfeffer 1975; Zimmerman and Zeitz 2002; Lane et al. 2013). Meyer and Rowan (1977) state that organizational survival (success) is linked to legitimacy and depends on the support the organization receives from its different constituencies. Therefore, our research aims to answer this research question: What strategies do the IUs use to gain legitimacy in China?

THEORETICAL FRAMEWORK: LEGITIMACY AND STRATEGIES TO GAIN LEGITIMACY

We combine Scott's (1995) and Suchman's (1995) legitimacy theories to examine how these institutions gain their legitimacy in China. Scott (1995) pointed out that legitimacy is not a commodity to be possessed or exchanged, but "a condition reflecting cultural alignment, normative support, or consonance with relevant rules or laws" (Scott 1995, 45). He suggests that legitimacy is composed of three pillars:

1. Regulative legitimacy: Organizations need to conform to the legally sanctioned regulations, laws, and rules to build their legitimacy from the government.
2. Normative legitimacy: An organization's practices and activities must be morally governed and appropriate to a specified purpose in order to be considered legitimate.
3. Cognitive legitimacy: Organizations must adopt an orthodox or "taken-for-granted" (Scott 1995, 47) structure or identity in order to gain legitimacy within society and to be viewed as doing things in a culturally correct way.

Suchman (1995) took a similar approach, though his terminology is different. He first defines legitimacy as "a generalized perception or assumption that the actions of an entity are desirable, proper, or appropriate within some socially constructed system of norms, values, beliefs and definitions" (Suchman 1995,574). Suchman suggested that organizations seek legitimacy to ensure stability and that their organizational activities are comprehensible. Legitimacy therefore results in organizations being "more meaningful, more predictable, and more trustworthy" (Suchman 1995, 575). Suchman (1995) then classified legitimacy into three types: pragmatic, moral, and cognitive. Pragmatic legitimacy refers to the self-interests of an organization's most immediate audiences and stakeholders. There are three subtypes within pragmatic legitimacy: Exchange legitimacy refers to constituents' support for an organizational policy based on that policy's expected value to them; Influence legitimacy gains constituents' support for the organization because it is responsive to their larger interests; and Dispositional legitimacy in which constituents view the organizations as individuals, and are likely to confer legitimacy to those organizations that have our best interests at heart, are decent, and wise. The second type of legitimacy, moral legitimacy, is concerned with whether the activity conducted by an organization is the right thing to do. More specifically, moral legitimacy is about whether the activity effectively promotes societal welfare, as defined by the audience's socially constructed value system. Moral legitimacy, which parallels Scott's normative pillar of institutions, involves evaluations of outputs and consequences, techniques and procedures, and categories and structure. Cognitive legitimacy, the third type of legitimacy in Suchman's theory, may involve either active and affirmative backing for an organization or mere acceptance of the organization as necessary or inevitable based on some taken-for-granted cultural account.

Legitimacy is not typically thought of as a binary feature of organizations, but a continuum. Legitimacy can be gained from various sources, and different thresholds of legitimacy apply (Kinser 2007). However, the literature lacks any operationalization of a legitimacy threshold, which would be difficult to measure in any case. Levy (2007) described the amount of legitimacy different organizations need to sustain survival and development:

Different organizations may draw from all, most, some, or just a few sources of legitimacy. This is sometimes a matter of choice, sometimes of necessity, and often a mix of the two. In any event, the number of sources is not fully correlated with the amount of legitimacy received from sources. Meyer and Scott (1983, 202) argued that the 'legitimacy of a given organization is negatively affected by the number of different authorities' sovereign over it and by the diversity or inconsistency of their accounts of how it is to function.' Some sources provide much more legitimacy than others. This depends not only on the source but also on the recipient. Thus a source dynamic that provides ample legitimacy to one institution may have little impact on another. Much here turns on the nature of the institution or sector, as well as on broader matters of the context within which higher education functions. At the same time, not all institutions require the same aggregate contribution from sources to have adequate legitimacy. (Levy 2007, 6)

Suchman (1995) further explained that legitimacy-building strategies roughly fall into three categories: (1) efforts to conform to the dictates of preexisting audiences within the organization's current environment; (2) efforts to select among multiple environments in pursuit of an audience that will support current practices; and (3) efforts to manipulate environmental structure by creating new audiences and new legitimating beliefs. Ahlstrom et al. (2008) did research on how private firms successfully gained legitimacy in an emerging economy such as China and discovered an interesting fourth strategy to gain legitimacy: helping to create the regulatory environment. Newly established organizations can create the rules and regulations for an industry if they are the pioneers in this area, and there is lack of government regulation. They can create norms and standards for the entire industry, sometimes in concert with government and other firms through collective action and self-regulation.

METHODOLOGY

Following the theoretical frameworks of Scott and Suchman, then, we examine three Chinese-foreign partnerships that represent different types and different stages of international university development. Specifically, we are interested in understanding what strategies these institutions use to gain their legitimacy in China. These three institutions are Xi'an Jiaotong Liverpool University (XJLTU), University of Nottingham Ningbo China (UNNC), and New York University Shanghai (NYU Shanghai). Both XJTLU and UNNC have been in operation more than five years, which we identify as a threshold for the new organizations' survival. NYU Shanghai is a new institution that began in 2013. XJTLU and UNNC are universities established by UK institutions, and NYU Shanghai is an U.S. institution. Similar to most Chinese-foreign partnerships, both Liverpool University and NYU have partnered with public universities, while University of Nottingham partnered with a private institution in China, Zhejiang Wanli University.

Interviews are the major data collection method we employed. Forty-two interviews were conducted with presidents, vice presidents, senior administrators, faculty, parents and students, and employers about these three IUs. In addition, experts on CCRS and government officials were also interviewed to have a thorough understanding of the legitimacy issues with these institutions.

In addition, we collected documentation, including memoranda, minutes of meetings, progress reports, formal studies or evaluations related to the cases, news clippings, and other articles appearing in the mass media or in community newspapers. The most important function of documentary evidence was to corroborate and augment evidence from other sources. We also attended a total of three conferences on CCRS held in China over the data collection period. Even though most of the presentations were self-promoting, we were able to interview some key people in this field to help us understand the legitimacy issues the international institutions faced.

FINDINGS

Chinese regulation[3] states that Chinese-foreign partnerships serve the following functions to:

1. borrow foreign expertise and to import high quality education resources;
2. accelerate China's education opening-up process to the world;
3. explore multiple approaches for developing student talent;
4. narrow the education gap between China and the developed countries;
5. improve the governance of the Chinese HEIs;
6. strengthen the development of the disciplinary programs at Chinese HEIs in order to meet the ever-growing demand for quality higher education;
7. cultivate global citizens who can understand and tolerate diverse cultures and work with people from diverse backgrounds; and
8. serve as an experiment and pilot program for the higher education reform in China.

The CCRS ventures, especially IUs, are expected to have these many functions in the Chinese higher education system and society. Indeed, this is the basis for their establishment; the authorization from the Chinese government gives them legal status from the start. In addition, the fact that the new IUs are usually established by world-class universities in the United Kingdom and United States, as well as prestigious Chinese government institutions, means that these institutions are not fly by-night operations. Legitimacy, however, cannot be assumed simply because IUs continue to exist under some government oversight and authority. The following sections will outline what each legitimacy pillar is in China, and analyze the strategies our case institutions use to gain legitimacy. Zimmerman and Zeitz (2002) suggest that conformance to the environment is the easiest strategy, while creating the environment is the most challenging strategy. The findings section, the strategies to gain legitimacy, will be presented in the order from the easiest to the most challenging.

Regulative Legitimacy and Strategies to Gain Regulative Legitimacy

Regulative legitimacy is commonly understood as the rules, regulations and laws that govern institutions. Scott (1995) specifies that regulative processes involve three parts: (1) rule setting: the capacity to establish rules, laws, and regulations; (2) monitoring: inspect or review other's conformity to the rules; and (3) sanctioning activities, which can manipulate sanctions through rewards or punishments to influence future behavior. These processes may operate through informal mechanisms, such as shaming or shunning activities; or through formal mechanisms, such as acts of a legally designated oversight body.

In China, the formal power of conferring regulative legitimacy to the IUs resides in the Ministry of Education (MoE), with the Department of International Cooperation and Exchanges (Office for Hong Kong, Macao, and Taiwan Affairs) being the implementing body. MoE regulatory functions follows each of three parts identified by Scott (1995). First, in setting the rules, MoE has issued several regulations and rules regarding the establishment, authorization, license, certificate registration and accreditation, and evaluation of CCRS. Second, MoE monitors the performance of CCRS, having developed indicators and processes to evaluate institutional mission, management systems, assets and financial management, quality, faculty, infrastructure, and social benefits. MoE assessment includes self-evaluation and field evaluation conducted by MoE officials and experts in the field. Third, MoE has the power to sanction programs, including demanding changes in the institution to correct deficiencies and closing inadequate programs. Given this power of the government, it is no surprise that institutions put great emphasis on gaining regulative legitimacy. The IUs in our study employed the following strategies for regulative legitimacy.

Strategy #1: Comply with the Environment

The most obvious way for the IUs to gain regulative legitimacy is to comply with the regulations and laws regarding CCRS. For example, all have Chinese presidents and a Chinese-majority Executive Board. These institutions' leaders state that they face so many uncertainties about their long-term development ahead, and their long-term sustainability could not be guaranteed at this point. Therefore, they rely on the national policy to protect them as they develop and improve themselves. The goal, then, is not simply to align with policies in order to gain the authorization to operate. Rather they wish to gain the favor of the regulatory agencies. This policy alignment, in other words, is not only required by the government, but is also a proactive way to be legitimate in the eyes of the government (X. J. Zhang, interview, March 16, 2015, in Jiangsu).

Strategy #2: Manipulate the Environment

However, the policy environment is difficult to formally change. In lieu of trying to change policies, some institutions have been figuring out new ways to work within the existing environment to create a preferable environment for their development. XJTLU provides a good example of this. In China, MoE requires an institution to be in operation for a certain number of years in order to offer doctoral degree programs. XJTLU failed to meet this requirement. So XJTLU took advantage of their connections with Liverpool University and decided to only provide doctoral degrees from Liverpool University at its China campus, rather than offering the degrees from XJTLU itself. In this manner, XJTLU was able to offer its students access to a doctoral degree even as it remained ineligible to offer the degree as a Chinese institution (Y. M. Xi, interview, March 15, 2015, in Jiangsu).

A more sensitive issue occurs with respect to the national government concerns that western values and cultures will lead to the corruption of traditional Chinese culture and values. Chinese leaders are protective of China's education sovereignty—their control over the educational system within the country–thus they impose tight ideological control in China. The senior leaders from the foreign institutions usually respond with caution and concerns, while their Chinese counterparts take it as a given. The tension is not easily resolved. Most IUs, in fact, have their own Chinese Communist Party Committee to deal with the students' ideological and political training, party building, and Chinese culture transmission. However, these Party Committees function differently from similar entities at Chinese universities. For example, even the most elite Chinese universities will immediately endorse and support national policies the moment that the policies come out in order to demonstrate their correct political orientation. This is not the case at IUs. Leaders at these institutions claim that their aim is to improve the home and the host institutions instead of favoring the government. Therefore, even though the international institutions maintain their regulative legitimacy, they are able to act differently than Chinese universities (X. J. Zhang, interview, March 16, 2015, in Jiangsu).

Strategy #3: Create the Environment

The policy regarding CCRS ventures in China has two realities. First, the policies often lag the actual practices of the IUs. Second, the policies are vague, meaning they can be interpreted with flexibility. These two features allow IU leaders to push for policy interpretations that are more favorable to their preferred practices. For example, the IU leaders view the current regulations and laws regarding CCRS as dated since they are oriented toward the traditional Chinese HEIs. IUs are highly regulated in terms of the student enrollment, tuition setting, degree program offering, and faculty promotion. The institutions' leaders perceive that their institutional development is confined by these regulations (Y. M., Xi, interview, March 15, in Jiangsu; W. Q. Shen, interview, April 2, 2015, in Ningbo). Therefore, the IUs usually try to influence government officials who interpret the rules through several different venues. For instance, they communicate with the government officials about their challenges when these officials visit them. The local government also aligns with the IUs to solicit support from the provincial and/or national government. Some of the foreign leaders from the home institutions are also members of the State Administration of Foreign Experts Affairs, the agency responsible for certifying foreign experts to work in China. Through this body, these leaders seek to influence the development of internationalization of higher education in China. Finally, in order to exert stronger impact, the IUs joined together to form the Sino-Foreign Cooperative University Union (SFCUU). The SFCUU serves as a venue for IUs to express their opinions and make themselves heard, and to solicit support, especially policy support for the development of their member institutions.

Normative Legitimacy and Strategies to Gain Normative Legitimacy

Normative legitimacy refers to the normal way that institutions operate, and the kinds of activities typically performed by other organizations in a similar institutional field. This often leads to isomorphism, in that normative legitimacy tends to push institutions into similar functions and, therefore, similar organizational structures. However, the ability of the IUs to act differently is often taken as a point of pride and distinctiveness when it comes to the education program. IUs specifically reject, in fact, certain norms practiced at the Chinese public HEIs, which include

(1) four years of disciplinary education; (2) treating students as children; (3) passive teaching and learning; (4) faculty's emphasis on research, rather than on teaching; and (5) the parallel political administrative structure at the Chinese HEIs. Accordingly, the IUs boast of their unique differences in (1) general education, (2) treating students as adults, (3) student-centered teaching and learning, (4) emphasis on faculty teaching, and (5) administrative professionalism.

General Education

In rejecting the four years a discipline-based education, IUs instead ground their undergraduate degrees in general education. In Chinese, this is termed 博雅教育 (*bo ya jiao yu*). UNNC former President Professor Fujia Yang provided his interpretation of *bo ya jiao yu*, which can be seen as similar to the perspective at other IUs. *Bo* refers to the broad and enriching education at IUs that includes both arts and sciences, instead of either arts or sciences. *Ya* means that the education the college students get should be advanced and sophisticated. Jiao refers to teaching and the emphasis on the professors as teachers. This not only focuses on the traditional classroom, but also emphasizes the education students get outside of the classroom. This perspective also recognizes that sometimes the latter is more important than the former. *Yu* emphasizes the importance of the process the students by which students are educated, and not just whether or not students have memorized facts.

Treating Students as Adults

In traditional Chinese HEIs, college students are treated as children, and the institutions serve as their guardians. However, at the IUs, students are treated as young adults. For example, the students have privacy over their grades, and the institutions refuse to disclose their grades to the parents. The IUs arrange fewer classes for the students compared to the Chinese universities, and the institutions do not regulate students outside of the classroom as much as the Chinese universities do. Thus the students at the IUs are expected to be more self-disciplined and independent.

Student-Centered Teaching and Learning

Unlike the instructor-centered lecture style of teaching at Chinese universities, at the IUs, the class size is much smaller, and students have more opportunities to interact with the professors. The students are encouraged to participate in classroom discussions as well as to ask questions. The students at the IUs are evaluated in multiple aspects, including class participation, assignments and projects, quizzes and tests, while the students at the Chinese HEIs are evaluated by mid- and final-term scores.

Emphasis on Faculty Teaching

At the traditional Chinese HEIs, faculty are evaluated by the number of their publications and the projects they are working on, rather than being assessed by their teaching. Also, the faculty's bonus is tied to their research productivity. Therefore, faculty are not incentivized to focus on teaching. The opposite is the case at the IUs. Faculty accentuate the importance of their teaching and students' learning. They invest heavily on students' learning experience at their institutions.

Administration Professionalism

Administration professionalism is another element that sets these institutions apart from traditional Chinese institutions. The selection of public university leaders, like the president and some middle-level management positions, is made by the government, and they have an equivalent governmental rank. For instance, the president of a prestigious university ranks the same as the minister of a governmental body, and the vice presidents or the deans rank the same as the city or county mayors. The majority of the administrators and faculty are Communist Party of China (CPC) members, with very few exceptions, and they are incentivized to move up the political ladder. At the IUs, they implement administrative professionalism. There are no equivalent governmental titles for the senior leadership at these IUs, and all are appointed under contracts with the university, not the government. Therefore their position relies on providing the students with real learning experiences and a high quality student life. It is an institutionally focused professional model, not a government-focused political model.

Because the IUs explicitly reject many normative activities in Chinese higher education, they need to make a special effort to gain and maintain normative legitimacy. This is particularly the case when they are dealing with parents of the students who have certain expectations of universities in China. For example, the parents have a difficult time understanding why these IUs charge more tuition but do less teaching than the public institutions (X. J. Zhang, interview, March 16, in Jiangsu). The IUs in our study employed the following strategies for normative legitimacy.

Strategy #1: Manipulate the Environment

The first strategy is to use their home institutions to explain some of their practices, especially when parents ask about their privacy policy and their student management. The IUs emphasize that they are either branch campus of or closely related to the foreign institution, therefore, they need to comply with the common practices at the home institutions regarding student privacy and management. Because the foreign institution is considered to be world-class, this strategy seeks to leverage the legitimacy of the foreign entity to promote the practices in China (Y. M., Xi, interview, March 15, in Jiangsu; W. Q. Shen, interview, April 2, 2015, in Ningbo).

Strategy #2: Create the Environment

The second strategy the international university leaders use is to take advantage of multiple communication outlets to help parents understand and support their practices. They use social media to promote their unique methods, and use personal meetings with parents to emphasize the international education model. For example, the senior leadership team, including the president, usually meets with the parents in person to answer their questions and concerns (Y. M., Xi, interview, March 15, in Jiangsu; Q. J. Xie, interview, March 16, 2015, in Suzhou; X. J. Zhang, interview, March 16, in Jiangsu). These IUs also use the attention they have from the public and the media to seize every opportunity to stress these new norms and practices at their universities. This has created a created a preferable environment for the public to understand and accept their practices.

Normative legitimacy emphasizes on the right thing to do and it involves evaluations of outputs and consequences, techniques and procedures, and category and structure (Scott 1995; Suchman 1995). The international university leaders believe what they are doing now is the right thing to do and call for Chinese universities to follow their lead. These aforementioned five dimensions of what a college education should be similar to can be considered as techniques and procedures, in Suchman and Scott's terms, of an organization. The international university leaders promote their education ideals and vision to the public, emphasizing that they are doing important work and making history in this era. More importantly, they believe that they are doing the right thing by providing a high-quality education and taking students' development and learning as the core of their operation.

In addition, the IUs demonstrate to the public that they have normative legitimacy in terms of outputs and consequences. Their graduates are their best outputs. The majority of the graduates of IUs continue their study in the world-renowned universities, or work for international companies. These outcomes are considered highly valuable in the Chinese society (X. Y. Guo, interview, March 10, 2015, in Nanjing).

Cognitive Legitimacy and Strategies to Gain Cognitive Legitimacy

Cognitive legitimacy is concerned with the nature of an organization being taken for granted. To apply this concept to the higher education institutions, this means that the IUs need to provide a trustworthy education that is worth what is being paid. The IUs enjoy a high profile stature when they are first established due to their nature of collaborating with well-known foreign institutions and the role they are expected to play to in the Chinese higher education arena. They have garnered spotlight attention from national and international leaders, corporations, scholars, and experts on higher education.

However, the IUs are still new institutions, and they have to work hard to gain recognition from society. At the very beginning, people said that they had never heard of these IUs. The initial impression, in fact, of XJTLU and UNNC was that they were third-tier universities because they were very different from the elite Chinese 985 and 211 project institutions. NYU Shanghai, because it was established later, had more credibility. But even as some people chose to believe that it was a fine institution, they had no idea why it was good. They wondered what was the difference between studying at NYU Shanghai and at the home campus, and whether NYU Shanghai was equivalent to the other prestigious universities in China, such as Tsinghua, Peking, or Fudan Universities (Y. M., Xi, interview, March 15, in Jiangsu; H. Meng, interview, March 20, 2015, Shanghai; March W. Q. Shen, interview, April 2, 2015, in Ningbo).

During the first few years of their operation, before their first generation of graduates, it was very difficult to recruit students. For example, the first cohort of 160 students who attended Xi'an Jiaotong Liverpool University, the president Professor Youmin Xi stated that it was a gamble for the parents. Even the admissions staff at XJTLU told the parents that they applauded their courage in choosing XJTLU because there might be risks bearing with this decision. The parents, on the other hand, knew their children would not be eligible to attend a first-tier Chinese university, yet they could get into a school that was associated with a world-class international university. Therefore the choice to attend XJTLU was not because they were confident in the school, but because it was potentially the best option available to them. Still, it was a risk (Y. M., Xi, interview, March 15, in Jiangsu).

Since IUs are new institutions in China, they understand that the first step for them to gain cognitive legitimacy is by showing that they are indeed trustworthy universities. In fact, these IUs have been trying to show the public that they are better universities than the public institutions in China. They have used several strategies to emphasize their cognitive legitimacy.

Strategy #1: Quality of Education and State-of-Art Facilities

IUs claim that they provide better quality of education than the public institutions do because they truly emphasize teaching and student development. They make several specific arguments for why their model of education is superior. They teach in English. They evaluate students based on multiple measures and not just tests. Their faculty are world-class, hired globally according to the home institution's standards. They rely on the foreign institutions and high quality administration for curricular excellence. They have better teaching facilities, and allow for greater measures of academic freedom (H. Meng, interview, March 20, 2015, Shanghai).

Academic freedom and student participation is particularly important. For example, Yang Fujia, the former Chancellor of UNNC, emphasizes that students are free to ask any questions and they could debate anything. Every student has the opportunity to ask questions in the classroom. They made every student participate in class discussion, and taught students to think critically and to work in teamwork. They made students the leader of learning in the classroom, the same as the learning style of Socrates. Although this is not taken for granted in China, it is in the foreign university. So this is used to emphasize the legitimacy of the foreign model in China.

Strategy #2: Create the Environment: Catfish Effect

The catfish effect is a Chinese expression that refers to how strong competition makes weaker entities better.[4] To apply this concept into the higher education field, the IUs invigorate the Chinese higher education institutions and improve their quality of education, especially their teaching. The IUs believe they have an impact on Chinese higher education system. Almost all the IUs have established or been thinking of establishing a research center on higher education innovation in China. XJTLU, for example, has a research center named Institute of Leadership and Educational Advanced Development (ILEAD). ILEAD has organized training programs through this Institute to serve as a great outlet for the public institutions in the province to get to know them. For instance, when Hunan University sent their first cohort of 20 newly recruited faculty members to XJTLU, they questioned what kind of institution it would be and why they should receive training there. After the training program, they were very impressed with what XJTLU offered to students, and ultimately sent 60 faculty members the second year (Y. M. Xi, interview, March 15, 2015, in Jiangsu; X. J. Zhang, interview, March 16, 2015, in Jiangsu).

The role and status of the IUs are evolving, especially XJTLU and UNNC. The local traditional Chinese higher education institutions are feeling the pressure imposed by the IUs. Students went to the universities with similar grades four years ago, but graduated with a totally different future—most of the graduates from IUs will continue their further education in western countries, while graduates from traditional Chinese universities either continue their study in China or enter the workforce. As one leader of an international university commented, "I often communicate with teachers from Ningbo University. Sometimes I get the sense that they are panic for their poor capability for running a university. They praise our university a lot and are very glad to come here to learn things and consult us more or less on issues like improving their teaching quality and educational reform" (W. Q. Shen, interview, April 2, 2015, in Ningbo).

This perspective, however, is not universally felt. Some Chinese scholars say that these IUs have limited effects. While they acknowledge the efforts made by the IUs, they don't believe that the IUs will bring earthshaking changes to other universities in such a short term and they have to wait for a long time to see the reform in the Chinese higher education system to come (L. Ye, interview, March 11, 2015, in Hangzhou; L. F. Li, interview, March 24, 2015, in Nanjing). Nevertheless, this is what the IUs are pushing, and are part of the legitimacy claim they make.

Strategy #3: Distinctiveness

The IUs view themselves on par with the top 10–20 universities in China (S. Morgan, interview, March 31, 2015, in Ningbo). More importantly, they see themselves as being unique, offering a product that is an international education and a prestigious western university degree. Overall, they are trying to develop a western education in China in English, using English language media. They perceive they have been very successful transplanting the home institution culture and way of education to China. At the same time, each of these IUs is unique with its own mission and positioning. The distinctiveness of each of our case institutions follows.

XJTLU consists of Xi'an Jiaotong University and Liverpool University, as indicated by its name. XJTLU states that they are not a branch campus of Liverpool University, but rather an independent institution that combines the advantages of three different models in the world: (1) American education: an emphasis on liberal arts education, (2) British education: strong quality control system, and (3) Chinese education: very practical and knowledge based. Another unique part of the program is the peer-mentor system at XJTLU that helps the new students adjust their life. The societal mentors are composed of some well-known entrepreneurs, who advise students on their career and job employment. Students also have a life mentor as well as an academic mentor.

The most distinctive character of XJTLU is in its new forms of university management. University leaders first proposed XJTLU as a networking organization, in which the units and departments of the university are loosely coupled together. The difference between a networking organization and a bureaucratic or matrix organization is that in the networking organization, the governance structure is flat, rather than hierarchical. Everybody knows their role and each role is supportive of the other roles to make it a holistic institution. The networking organization emphasizes each individual's self-motivation rather than individuals needing supervised.

IUs, in essence, are a combination of western and Chinese ideals, values, and norms, which can be drastically different. How to make the institutions sustainable can be very challenging, especially in the Chinese society full of uncertainties, ambiguities, complexities, and changes at light speed. XJTLU proposes harmony management, quite similar to the old Chinese way of yin and yang. Leaders have, in fact, adapted Mintzberg's art-science-craft triangle style

CHINESE-FOREIGN COOPERATION IN RUNNING SCHOOLS

management to a new XJTLU five-star style management, including art-experience-philosophy-science-craft (techniques). The five-star model combines the western emphasis on experiments, analysis and quantity formula description with the Chinese philosophical stress on harmony and cooperation.

The distinctive element of NYU Shanghai relate to its international student body. Half the undergraduates come from China, and half come from the rest of the world. Every Chinese student has a non-Chinese roommate, and vice versa. Every day students experience an intense education by living and studying in a multicultural world.

A second distinctive characteristic is in how NYU Shanghai delivers an undergraduate liberal education in the humanities, social sciences, and natural sciences, promoting the skills of critical and creative thinking. All of NYU Shanghai undergraduate students will pursue a core curriculum in Shanghai for the first two years, and then spend their junior year studying at other NYU campuses in New York and Abu Dhabi or global academic centers in eleven other cities around the world. The students then return to Shanghai to complete their degrees.

A third distinctive characteristic is how NYU Shanghai selects its potential students. All the international students have to apply through NYU Shanghai's office in New York. Soft skills and personality determine which campus students will be accepted. There is a Chinese admission team specifically focused on applicants who are Chinese citizens. For Chinese students who apply for NYU Shanghai, they have to go through several major steps: (1) apply through NYU general application system; (2) provide high school transcripts; and (3) after review the first two rounds of application materials, eligible students are invited to attend Candidate Weekend, which composes of six sessions: hotel registration, dinner with faculty and leadership team (English-only environment), 20-second speech about a object, interview, demo class, and group activities. Students are evaluated mainly by three parts: the participation in the demo class, faculty recommendation, and evaluators. Then conditional admission will be offered to students. These conditionally admitted students have to take the Chinese College Entrance Examination and only if they score higher than the cut-off points for first-tier universities, will they be officially accepted by NYU Shanghai.

The UK side of UNNC is mainly responsible for academic governance, whereas the Chinese counterpart takes charge of Chinese culture and student services. The distinctive aspect is that the whole teaching system intends to be the same as that of University of Nottingham. The senior leadership team of the Nottingham University claims that the three campuses of the Nottingham[5] are a whole family. The website design is the same. They have the same system, and the content is consistent over the three campuses. If UNNC students study at the home campus, their ID will automatically be transferred to the system at the home campus. UNNC is part of the Nottingham University overall strategy.[6]

All three IUs seek to be unique to separate themselves from the traditional Chinese higher education institutions, as well as among themselves. They see the weaknesses of the traditional universities, even within the world first-class universities, which gives these institutions confidence as well as provides them an opportunity to be on par with the world-class universities. The IUs call it the late-mover advantages. They believe that the traditional universities need to be reconstructed, which the IUs can provide such a solution because they do not have historic burden, so they can build up an excellent university without many constraints. More importantly, the IUs want to be leaders and pioneers of higher education, rather than followers. In the Chinese higher education arena, just because the IUs are new institutions with high expectations, they have first-mover advantage in achieving what they plan to change in the Chinese higher education system.

Pragmatic Legitimacy and Strategies to Gain Pragmatic Legitimacy

Organizations gain pragmatic legitimacy by meeting the needs of their most immediate audiences and stakeholders. The IUs have several major categories of stakeholders in China, including government, students and parents, employers, and the host institution. We label these as tangible stakeholders, because they are explicitly acknowledged groups that directly influence the development of IUs. Parents, students, and governments are the most immediate stakeholders because they determine the survival and development of these institutions. The IUs in China are primarily considered as private institutions. Even though they have a high profile in the higher education sector, and substantial political support overall, they receive no financial support from the national government or the provincial government. The local government usually foots the bill for the universities' infrastructure and the first few years of operation. Therefore, they rely heavily on the market in order to survive and prosper, and must convince parents and students that they are a worthwhile investment. Employers are a stakeholder for the IUs, but not as essential as parents or the government because the majority of the students pursue further education abroad after their graduation.

Parents and Students

Parents and students confer all the three subtypes of pragmatic legitimacy to these institutions, as summarized by Suchman (1995). Parents provide exchange legitimacy when they trade their support for the IUs in exchange for a better future for their children after four years of study. In addition, parents and students provide Influence Legitimacy as avid supporters of IUs and they use their status to convince others of the value of IUs as an example of higher education reform in China. Finally, because they view IUs as doing something different and, in fact, better than the traditional Chinese public institutions because of their affiliation with prestigious western universities, parents and student give dispositional legitimacy to the Chinese-foreign partnerships. They use multiple outlets to promote the IUs.

It is important to note the double identities parents have as stakeholders. One is that they confer legitimacy to the international institutions by sending their children there. The other is that they actively help these institutions to gain legitimacy from the society. When the IUs were first established, the parents and students had no idea about what these institutions would provide them. The institutions had to work hard to demonstrate that they were trustworthy institutions that were able to provide much better quality of education. The placement of graduates was therefore the most important feature of these institutions.

The majority of the undergraduates of XJTLU and UNNC choose to pursue further education abroad, mainly in United Kingdom, the United States and Australia. Among 838 graduates of XJTLU in 2014, for example, 837 students chose to study abroad while only one student decided to continue his graduate education in China (T. Lin, interview, March 16, 2015, in Jiangsu). At UNNC, three fourths of the graduates further their study and nearly all of the rest are employed within a few months of graduation. The graduates voluntarily become spokesperson for the school out of appreciation for the education they received, and their parents voluntarily promote these institutions in multiple ways, including communicating with the high schools where their children graduated from and promoting these institutions through marketing channels. When the admissions staff at these IUs go on recruitment tours in other cities, the local parents will voluntarily host them and help them promote their institutions in the local area (L. Y. Sun, interview, April 1, 2015, in Ningbo). Because many of these parents are elites and well-educated in the Chinese society, they can be very influential. Current students are often invited to go on the recruitment tours with the admissions staff at these institutions. The prospective students and parents believe that it is far more reliable to hear from the students than from the admissions staff. The parents and students have been helping the institutions build their reputation through word of mouth referral (Q. J. Xie, interview, March 16, 2015, in Jiangsu; L. Y. Sun, interview, April 1, 2015, in Ningbo).

Local Government

The local government is another important stakeholder for the IUs since it invests heavily in these international institutions. Local governments want to host IUs to attract education resources, technologies, highly educated human resources and to build their city brand to boost local economic development. The Shanghai government, for example, promised to provide financial support for NYU Shanghai for its first five years of operation. The government made a series of agreements with NYU Shanghai, including hiring high-quality and high profile faculty worldwide at least at the same level as the faculty of New York University in the United States. They made sure that students in Shanghai would be provided with the same resources as those at the home institution, and that the admissions standards at NYU Shanghai would be in line with the enrollment procedures and standards of New York University. The financial support from the Shanghai government ensured that NYU Shanghai could provide state-of-art facilities from the very beginning (H. Meng, interview, March 20, 2015, in Shanghai).

Strategy #1: Comply with the Environment

To gain legitimacy from the government, especially from the local government, the IUs offer degree programs that are compatible with the local economic needs. For example, Ningbo is a big seaport city in China and UNNC has established an Institute of Marine Economics that links local economy and business enterprises.

Strategy #2: Select the Environment

The IUs also select to locate in the economically developed regions in China, such as Shanghai, Shenzhen, Guangzhou, and Suzhou. There are multiple reasons for this decision. On the one side, local governments have economic needs and have opened up to the outside world and implemented economic reforms. This openness is a necessary prerequisite for many western universities to engage with international partners in China. Plus, because of previous efforts at economic development, these regions are adjusting their economic structure from labor-intensive to resource intensive. This requires new knowledge and skills. Moreover, these highly economic developed regions can afford to make large investments in the establishment and operation of the universities. Hence they provide preferential policy and financial support to attract the IUs to locate there.

Simply stated, IUs gain legitimacy by delivering on their promises made to the local government. NYU Shanghai, for example, is demonstrating to the local government that they are serious about providing high quality education. They invited 28 Nobel laureates as well as several members of the National Academy of Sciences in the United States to teach courses and deliver lectures on their China campus. The Shanghai government has been satisfied with these efforts so far and has been willing to provide additional support to NYU Shanghai as a result.

CONCLUSION

The focus of the IUs in China has been on establishing an operating institution, enrolling students, and gaining public support for their activities. Following the theories of Scott (1995) and Suchman (1995), we can also identify their efforts at gaining legitimacy as well. We initially identified the liabilities of newness and foreignness as barriers to the pursuit of legitimacy. The research into our three case examples suggests where these liabilities occur and where they have shown a somewhat different pattern.

Liability of Newness

The IUs all rely on an accommodating policy from the national government that has allowed them to open and build a unique educational program. But the government only opened the doors a little to this new initiative, and keeps tight rein on who is welcomed into China, and what the institutions are allowed to do. In addition, the leaders and supporters of the IUs have continually promoted their activities, reminding the public of what they do and how it is an important activity in China. They also continue to address skeptics of their form, both within China and from the international community, who wonder whether these new institutions represent the same quality of education as their famous partners. IUs clearly do not have the taken-for-granted legitimacy that Suchman (1995) suggest is an important benefit of long-standing organizations. The liability of newness in that respect is still much in evidence.

In other ways, however, the fact that they are new gives the IUs an ability to act with greater freedom. This, then, allows them to be positioned as needed reform for the Chinese system. As many parents and officials agree that reform is needed, the new institutions can be seen as being on the vanguard of the future of higher education. The Chinese institutions cannot make these changes, so the international institutions, as first-movers, are able to use this to their advantage. The evidence shows, in fact, that the parents and students who took the risk and first enrolled promoted the new model as something new and different, presenting this as an important advantage for others to consider.

Liability of Foreignness

The liability of foreignness suggests that organizations that come from the outside face greater scrutiny and have a more difficult time developing local legitimacy. Our research showed some evidence of this. Questions from parents, for example, suggested that the class size and smaller teaching loads were incompatible with the local expectations for higher education. The cost of the education also raised additional concerns. But perhaps the biggest impacts of this liability were in the requirements that a local university needed to be a senior partner, that Chinese citizens needs to be majority representation in the leadership, and that the institutions needed to serve mostly Chinese citizens. There was limited trust of the foreign entity, and much concern that the educational sovereignty of China should be protected.

Nevertheless, the liability of foreignness ended up having much less impact on the IUs than the theory suggests. The fact that the partnerships were with well-known foreign universities added credibility. And the emphasis on the reality that the universities were in fact Chinese institutions, in partnership with existing Chinese universities, was also very important. Each of our case institutions navigated this foreignness differently, however. As the oldest of the IUs, UNNC also was partnered with the only private Chinese institution, which meant that the local status of the Chinese partner was not very high. It therefore relied on the Chinese citizenship of the University of Nottingham President to alleviate concerns about foreignness. XJTLU emphasized the relationship with Xi'an Jiaotong University as an elite partner, putting the name of the Chinese institution first. NYU-Shanghai had perhaps the easiest time in this regard, focusing on its status as an elite American university with longstanding relationships in China. Even though it has a prestigious local partner in East China Normal University, it used its standing as a world-class university to make clear the education would be second to none. It is also important to note that as the newest IUs in our sample, NYU-Shanghai benefited greatly from the legitimacy already gained by its predecessors.

This study shows that even though the IUs might carry over some amount of legitimacy from their home institution, government policies need to be supportive for them to gain legitimacy. And even with regulative legitimacy in place, the organizations still have to work hard to gain other dimensions of legitimacy in order to survive and thrive.

The literature on organizations' strategies to gain legitimacy has been mainly derived from Suchman (1995) and Scott (1995), which focus on the organizations using different strategies to create preferable external environment for their organizational survival and development. Our research shows that legitimacy theory provides a relevant perspective on the establishment of branch campuses. In particular we find that the socially constructed external environment is indeed important for the organizations to gain legitimacy. The core of the higher education organization–the quality of the product–becomes the leading strategy for the organizations to gain legitimacy from different stakeholders. To be more specific, the legitimacy of these IUs derived significantly from their ability to argue successfully that the quality of education they provided was better than other options. Their most immediate stakeholders–parents and students, the local government and employers–consistently referenced quality, and the institutions themselves never wavered from their quality claims. How each international university hires and maintains a high quality faculty is relevant here. All argued that their faculty in China were comparable to the faculty on the home campus. They relied, however, on a core faculty that was hired specifically to teach in China, with a few individuals who were either seconded from the home campus, or who traveled to China for short periods to teach before returning back home. Yet by promoting their faculty as world class, even as they were hired locally, the IUs could sustain their claim to a better educational program than their local competitors.

CHINESE-FOREIGN COOPERATION IN RUNNING SCHOOLS

This is an important caveat to the study of legitimacy. It is dependent on organizational activities. If the quality of the IUs slips, or if it is shown to not be as good as it claims, the legitimacy would likely quickly fall away. This conclusion, therefore, holds important lessons for those who seek to establish the permanent legacy of these institutions in China as the forerunners of innovation for the entire system.

NOTES

1. An organization that has legal person status is considered an independent legal entity.
2. Cross-Border Education Research Team (C-BERT) uses a definition of branch campus that excludes 26 of the international colleges.
3. Regulation on CCRS and its implement measures.
4. This originates in the idea that a catfish in a school of sardines forces the sardines to keep active and strong.
5. Nottingham has another branch campus in Malaysia.
6. The campus itself also reflects this, as the distinctive Nottingham clock tower dominates the campus in England and in China.

REFERENCES

Ahlstrom, D., G. D. Bruton, and K. S. Yeh. (2008). Private firms in China: Building legitimacy in an emerging economy. *Journal of World Business* 43:385–400.

Becker, R. F. J. 2009. *International branch campuses: Markets and strategies.* London: Observatory on Borderless Higher Education. http://www.obhe.ac.uk/documents/view_details?id=770

Bianchi, C. C., and E. Ostale. 2006. Lessons learned from unsuccessful internationalization attempts: Examples of multinational retailers in Chile. *Journal of Business Research* 59 (1):140–47. doi:10.1016/j.jbusres.2005.01.002

Borgos, J. E. 2013. Using principal-agent theory as a framework for analysis in the evaluating multiple stakeholders involved in the accreditation and quality assurance of international medical branch campuses. *Quality in Higher Education* 19 (2):173–90. doi:10.1080/13538322.2013.805068

Cheng, B., and Y. K. Cheng. 2007. Research summary on Chinese-foreign collaboration in running schools (CCRS) since 2000. *Academic Forum* 2:196–99.

Cross-Border Education Research Team. 2015. Branch campus listing. http://globalhighered.org/branchcampuses.php

Díez-Martín, F., C. Prado-Roman, and A. Blanco-González. 2013. Beyond legitimacy: Legitimacy types and organizational success. *Management Decision* 51 (10):1954–69. doi:10.1108/md-08-2012-0561

Dowling, J., and J. Pfeffer. 1975. Organizational legitimacy: Social values and organizational behavior. *Pacific Sociology Review* 18 (1):122–36. doi:10.2307/1388226

Farrugia, C. A., and J. E. Lane. 2013. Legitimacy in cross-border higher education: Identifying stakeholders of international branch campuses. *Journal of Studies in International Education* 17 (4):414–32. doi:10.1177/1028315312464379

Freeman, J., G. R. Carroll, and M. T. Hannan. 1983. The liability of newness: Age dependence in organizational death rates. *American Sociology Review* 48 (5):692–710. doi:10.2307/2094928

Kinser, K. (2007). Sources of legitimacy in U.S. for-profit higher education. In *Private higher education in post-communist Europe*, ed. S. Slantcheva and D. C. Levy 257–76. New York: Palgrave Macmillan.

Kostova, T., and S. Zaheer. 1999. Organizational legitimacy under conditions of complexity: The case of the multinational enterprise. *Academy of Management Review* 24 (1):64–81. doi:10.2307/259037

Lane, J. E., K. Kinser, and D. Knox. 2012. Regulating cross-border higher education: A case study of the united states. *Higher Education Policy* 26:147–12. doi:10.1057/hep.2012.23

Levy, D. C. 2007. Legitimacy and privateness: Central and eastern European private higher education in global context. In *Private higher education in post-communist Europe*, ed. S. Slantcheva and D. C. Levy, 279–98. New York: Palgrave Macmillan.

Meyer, J. W., and B. Rowan. 1977. Institutionalized organizations – Formal-structure as myth and ceremony. *American Journal of Sociology* 83 (2):340–63. doi:10.1086/226550

Meyer, J. W., and W. R. Scott. (1983). Centralization and the legitimacy problems of local government. In *Organizational environments: Ritual and rationality*, ed. J. W. Meyer, W. R. Scott, B. Rowan and T. E. Deal, 199–215. Thousand Oaks, CA: Sage.

Ministry of Education. 2015. Chinese-foreign cooperation in running schools. http://www.crs.jsj.edu.cn/index.php/default/index (accessed December 10, 2015).

Scott, W. R. 1995. *Institutions and organizations*. Thousand Oaks, California: Sage.

Singh, J. V., D. J. Tucker, and R. J. House. 1986. Organizational legitimacy and the liability of newness. *Administrative Science Quarterly* 31:171–93. doi:10.2307/2392787

Suchman, M. C. 1995. Managing legitimacy: Strategic and institutional approaches. *Academy of Management Review* 20 (3):571–610. doi:10.2307/258788

Tao, L., and J. L. Shen. 2006. A research summary of international cooperation of running branch schools in recent ten years. *Education of Chinese Medicine* 25 (4):5–10.

Vanhonacker, W. R. 2000. A better way to crack China. *Harvard Business Review* 78 (4):20–21.

Zaheer, S., and E. Mosakowski. 1997. The dynamics of the liability of foreignness: A global study of survival in financial services. *Strategic Management Journal* 18:439–63. doi:10.1002/(sici)1097-0266(199706)18:6<439::aid-smj884>3.3.co;2-p

Zimmerman, M. A., and G. J. Zeitz. 2002. Beyond survival: Achieving new venture growth by building legitimacy. *Academy of Management Review* 27 (3):414–31. doi:10.2307/4134387

Index

Abu Dhabi *see* comparative analysis of international branch campuses (IBCs) in China, Qatar and UAE
access and approval mechanisms 9–10, 19, 41, 42
accountability 13, 22, 64
accreditation 11–12, 17, 21
Acquaah, M. 52
adult education 7
Africa 52, 80
agreements 18, 40, 48, 61; 'withdrawal in the case of poor operations' in cooperative 13
agriculture 40
Ahlstrom, D. 99
Altbach, P. G. 44, 45, 56, 57, 60, 64, 84
applied technical education 36
approval and access mechanisms 9–10, 19, 41, 42
Argentina 17
Arimoto, A. 85
Asia 52; Eastern Asia's cross-border partnerships 61–2
Asian Development Bank 61
auditing 22
Australia 4, 16–17, 41, 45, 55, 78, 82, 109; quality assurance 5

basic relationships among scale, quality and benefits 26–42; applying theoretical framework 39–42; appropriate scale as foundation 33–6; controlling standards for access 41; exploring differentiated permissions 42; increased benefits as goal 38–9; innovative quality as key 36–7; key points for development 40–1; point of balance 39–40; policy points 40; public concerns 30–1; public opinion 32–3; theoretical framework 33–42
Becker, R. F. J. 45, 97
Belt and Road Initiatives 1, 36, 42
Bodycott, P. 84
Borgos, C. J. 52, 53, 54, 55, 56, 57

Borgos, J. E. 97
bottom-up strategies 61, 70
brands 71
Brazil 17
Brunsson, N. 62
business and management 68
business models 43; IBC *see* comparative analysis of international branch campuses (IBCs) in China, Qatar and UAE

Canada 78
capital investment 22–3
Carnegie Mellon University: Australia 55; Qatar 49, 55
catfish effect 106–7
'chain store' phenomenon 41
Chambers, G. S. 45
Chan, S. J. 80
Chang, H. 18
Chapman, D. W. 61
Chen, L. Y. 82
Chen, S. 85
Cheng, B. 97
Cheung Kong Graduate School of Business 28, 65
Chile 17
Chinese University of Hong Kong (CUHK) 64, 65; -Shenzhen 67
Choudaha, R. 39
Christensen, T. 62
City University of Seattle in Switzerland 54–5
class 69, 70, 81, 86
classified regulation mechanism 10–11
collective action and self-regulation 99
Communist Party of China 104
Communist Party Committee 70, 102
comparative analysis of international branch campuses (IBCs) in China, Qatar and UAE 43–57; adaptation 51–2, 57; business models 50–2, 56, 57; China 44, 46, 47–8, 51, 52, 53,

115

INDEX

54–5, 56–7, 97; defining IBC 45; governance and leadership 52–6; growth of IBCs 45–6; isomorphic patterns 51, 54; organizational perspective on IBC development 50–4; organizational structures, differences in 54–6, 57; Qatar 44, 46, 48–9, 51, 52, 53, 54, 55, 56–7; resource dependence theory 52, 53; social networks and relationships 52, 53; sustainability 50, 52, 53, 56–7; UAE 44, 46, 49–50, 51, 52, 53, 54, 56–7, 97; uncertainty 52, 53
Confucian tradition 69
consulates and embassies 10
continuing education 7
coordination and cooperation between departments 22
creativity 108; and problem awareness 8
Cross-Border Education Research Team 45, 46
cultural diversity 61, 100
cultural heritage 62
Cummings, W. K. 60

Deng Xiaoping 47
developing countries 17, 44, 45, 52; accreditation 12
DiMaggio, P. J. 51, 54, 61, 69
disciplines 10–11, 17, 29–30, 36, 38, 40, 65, 67, 68, 70–1, 81, 108
diversification 4, 5, 16–17, 18; concept of quality 9, 10
Dowling, J. 97
Dubai *see* comparative analysis of international branch campuses (IBCs) in China, Qatar and UAE
Duke University 4; Dubai 56; Duke Kunshan University 4, 34, 48, 63, 71

East China Normal University in Shanghai 48, 112
East China University of Science and Technology in Shanghai 66
Eastern Asia's cross-border partnerships 61–2
Eastern European countries 12
economics and management 67
economies of scale 33
Education Plan Outline (National Plan for Medium and Long-Term Education Reform and Development) (2010–20) 1, 5, 6, 8, 17, 19, 35
Egypt 17
embassies and consulates 10
employment rate 37
engineering 10–11, 17, 40, 67, 81
entrepreneurship 64
European Network for Quality Assurance in Higher Education (ENQA) 4–5

evaluation and accreditation mechanisms 11–12, 17, 21
exit/entry visas 22
experiential learning approach 69

Farrugia, C. A. 97
fees 4, 7, 13, 22, 34, 49, 69, 104, 112
Fegan, J. 61
Feng, Y. 48
financial support 22–3, 109
first-mover advantage 109, 111
Florida State University 45
for-profit education 20–1
foreign exchange 22, 23
Freeman, J. 97
Friese, S. 53
Fudan University 65
functions of Chinese-foreign partnerships 100

Garrett, R. 51
Geng, D. L. 82
Georgetown University School of Foreign Service 49
Glidden, R. 12
globalization 4, 47, 60, 61–2, 81, 86
Going Global development strategy 21, 35, 36
Gonzalez, G. C. L. 49
Granovetter, M. S. 52
grant foundations 23
growth models 35
Gu, J. X. 12

Hayhoe, R. 80
He, L. 80
high-quality educational resources 15–24; capital investment 22–3; categorized management 20–1; complementarity 17; coordination and planning mechanisms 21–2; diversity 16–17, 18; financial support 22–3; Going Global development strategy 21; guarantee measures for introduction of 19–22; key points 18–19; national socioeconomic development 18–19; practicality 17; proceduralization 18; regional development 18, 19; regional distribution 20; restructuring strategic distribution of 20; school capacity building 18; social environment 23; student based and career oriented 18; support systems for introduction of 22–4; training system for Sino-foreign cooperative education 24; *see also* basic relationships among scale, quality and benefits; quality improvement
Hong Kong Polytechnic University (PolyU) 64, 65, 66

INDEX

Hong Kong Shue Yan College (later University) 64, 65
Hong Kong University of Science and Technology (HKUST) 64; Joint School of Sustainable Development: Xian-Jiaotong University and 67
Hong Kong's cross-system university partnerships 60–71; China's cross-system engagement with overseas partners 62–3; Eastern Asia's cross-border partnerships 61–2; entrepreneurship 64; historical background 63–5; interactions between organization and environment 69–70; interorganizational interactions 68–9; joint campuses 67–70; knowledge economy 64; Parental Affairs Section 69–70; privatization 64; program-level collaboration 65–6; university governance in Hong Kong 63; value of case studies 62; whole-person education model 68–9, 70
Hopkins-Nanjing Center 55
Huang, F. 61, 80
Hughes, R. 57
humanities 11, 67, 68, 108
Hvistendahl, M. 47
hybridity 60

India 17, 80
indigenization 86
Indonesia 17
information technology (IT) 81
institutional theory 51, 54, 69
intercollegiate exchange programs 7, 40
international branch campuses (IBCs): comparative analysis of China, Qatar and UAE 43–57; adaptation 51–2, 57; business models 50–2, 56, 57; China 44, 46, 47–8, 51, 52, 53, 54–5, 56–7, 97; defining IBC 45; governance and leadership 52–6; growth of IBCs 45–6; isomorphic patterns 51, 54; organizational perspective on IBC development 50–4; organizational structures, differences in 54–6, 57; Qatar 44, 46, 48–9, 51, 52, 53, 54, 55, 56–7; resource dependence theory 52, 53; social networks and relationships 52, 53; sustainability 50, 52, 53, 56–7; UAE 44, 46, 49–50, 51, 52, 53, 54, 56–7, 97; uncertainty 52, 53
international law 11, 65
international trade 57
isomorphism 51, 54, 61, 69
Italy 45

Japan 85
Ji, B. C. 8
Johns Hopkins University 45, 55

joint venture IBC model 51
Jung, J. 85

Kean University 63
Kinser, K. 45, 50, 51, 57, 98
Knight, J. 45, 57, 60, 75
Korea 85
Kosmützky, A. 76, 80
Kostova, T. 97
Krieger, Z. 49

Lane, J. E. 43, 44, 45, 50, 51, 56, 57, 97
language 67, 82, 85, 106, 107, 108
late-mover advantages 108
Lawton, W. 45, 51
legal education 17; international law 11, 65
legitimacy quest of international universities 96–113; cognitive legitimacy 98, 105–9; conclusion 111–13; findings 100–11; functions of Chinese-foreign partnerships 100; legal person status 97; methodology 99–100; normative legitimacy 98, 102–5; pragmatic legitimacy 98, 109–11; regulative legitimacy 98, 100–2, 112; theoretical framework: legitimacy and strategies to gain legitimacy 98–9
Levy, D. C. 98–9
Li Ka Shing 65
Li, M. 81, 84
Li, X. 80
Li, X. H. 76
Lin, J. H. 3, 4, 5, 7, 11, 15, 16, 35, 82
literature review 75–86; authorship patterns 78–80, 85; average length of articles 84; citations 84, 89–95; discussion and conclusion 84–6; methodology 76–7; number of journal articles by year 77–8; number of references 84; research methods analysis 82–4, 86; thematic clusters 80–2, 85, 86
Liverpool University: Xi'an Jiaotong Liverpool University 63, 96, 99–113
local government see provincial and local governments
localization 86

Macau 65, 68
Malaysia 17
management: and business 68; and economics 67
Marginson, S. 60
media 32, 33
medicine 17, 40
Meng, Z. Y. 82
mentors 107
Meyer, J. W. 61, 69, 97

INDEX

middle class 69, 70, 81
Middle East 52; *see also* international branch
campuses (IBCs): comparative analysis of
China, Qatar and UAE
military training 70
Ministry of Education 9, 11, 13, 21, 30–1, 35–7,
39, 47, 48, 55, 65, 75, 97; authentication
platform 34; 'chain store' phenomenon 41;
Notice Regarding Strengthened Standards
Management in Foreign-Affiliated Education
(2012) 6; regulative legitimacy 101
Mo, Y. W. 82
Mok, K. H. 64
Moufahim, M. 81

Nanjing University 55
National Plan for Medium and Long-Term
Education Reform and Development (2010–20)
1, 5, 6, 8, 17, 19, 35
neoinstitutionalism 61
neoliberalism 69
networking organization 107
New York Institute of Technology (NYIT) 55
New York University: Abu Dhabi 56, 57; Shanghai
4, 34, 48, 57, 63, 71, 96, 99–113
New Zealand 4
Ng Ching-Fai 70
nonprofit education 20–1, 65, 67
Northwestern University 49, 57
Nottingham Ningbo China, University of (UNNC)
48, 63, 71, 96, 99–113
number of institutions, programs and students
27–8, 75–6
number of students enrolled in higher education 35

Obamba, M. 80
Observatory of Borderless Higher Education
(OBHE) 44, 45
OECD: Guidelines for Quality Provision in
Cross-Border Higher Education (jointly with
UNESCO) 4
Ong, L. C. 80
organizational behavior *see* international branch
campuses (IBCs): comparative analysis of
China, Qatar and UAE
overseas education 35–6

Pan, M. Y. 8, 60, 61, 63
Panama 45
path dependency 60, 62
peer-mentor system 107
Peking University (PKU) 65
penalization and withdrawal mechanisms 12–13, 35

Peng, M. W. 52
Pfeffer, J. 52, 57
Philippines 17
Pierson, P. 62
postgraduate programs 28, 30, 55, 65, 66, 71, 101
power relations 86
privacy 104
privatization 64
profit 20–1, 37, 41
provincial and local governments 9, 11, 19, 20,
21–2, 34, 41, 70; grant foundations 23;
legitimacy quest of international universities
109, 110, 111; ministry-province joint approval
mechanism 42; public opinion 23; training for
administrative personnel 24
public opinion 23, 32–3
publicity drive 23

Qatar *see* international branch campuses (IBCs):
comparative analysis of China, Qatar and UAE
Qin, M. Q. 81
quality *see* basic relationships among scale, quality
and benefits
quality improvement 3–13; approval and access
mechanisms 9–10; classified regulation
mechanism 10–11; correct concept of quality
8–9; creativity and problem awareness 8;
evaluation and accreditation mechanisms 11–12;
international trend 4–5; key advances and
existing problems 233–4; penalization and
withdrawal mechanisms 12–13; Sino-foreign
cooperative education: component part of
Chinese education 6–8

Ramirez, F. O. 62
rankings 4, 10, 16, 32, 41, 61–2, 63
reciprocal credit recognition 7, 40
Redden, E. 63
reform, educational (1980s) 47
regions 18, 19, 20, 28–9
relationships and social networks 52, 53
Renmin University 65
reputation 4, 32, 34, 40, 110
research on cross-border higher education in
China: literature review 75–86
research institutions 23, 24, 60, 71
resource dependence theory 52, 53
Rizvi, F. 81, 84

Sanyal, B. C. 12
scale *see* basic relationships among scale, quality
and benefits
science 10–11, 40, 67, 68, 71, 81

INDEX

Scott, J. 53
Scott, R. 52
Scott, W. R. 96, 98, 99, 100, 101, 105, 111, 112
self-regulation 99
Selznick, P. 62
Sichuan University 66
Singapore 12–13
Sino-Foreign Cooperative University Union (SFCUU) 102
social media 104
social networks 52, 53
social sciences 11, 67, 68, 108
Socrates 106
Solomon, D. A. 80
South Africa 17
sovereignty 48, 63, 82, 97, 101–2, 112
Stinchcombe, A. L. 62
strategic alliances (IBCs) 51, 55, 56
student-centered teaching and learning 103
study abroad 22, 37, 39, 47, 75, 81, 105, 106–7, 108, 109; preparatory courses 7, 40
Suchman, M. C. 96, 98, 99, 105, 109, 111, 112
Sun Yat-sen 64
Switzerland 55

Taiwan 65, 68, 80, 82
Tang, Z. F. 11
Tao, L. 76, 97
taxation 22, 23; tax-free zones in UAE 50, 56
teachers 8, 13, 22, 34, 36, 67, 82, 85, 103, 110, 111, 112; emphasis on faculty teaching 103–4
technology 68, 71
Texas A&M University 49
Thailand 17
Thelen, K. 62
Tierney, W. G. 60
Ting, J. S. P. 64
training system for Sino-foreign cooperative education 24
transitional economies 44, 52
transparency 22, 64
trial and error 42
Tsang, E. 69, 81
Tsinghua University 65

undergraduate programs 28, 30, 66, 67, 68, 103, 108
UNESCO: Guidelines for Quality Provision in Cross-Border Higher Education (jointly with OECD) 4
United Arab Emirates see international branch campuses (IBCs): comparative analysis of China, Qatar and UAE

United Kingdom 4, 5, 16–17, 39, 45, 78, 82, 100, 109
United States 4, 16–17, 41, 78, 82, 100, 109; IBCs see international branch campuses (IBCs): comparative analysis of China, Qatar and UAE; quality accreditation system 5, 12
University of Hong Kong (HKU) 64, 65
University of Montana 63
University of Nottingham Ningbo China (UNNC) 48, 63, 71, 96, 99–113

van der Wende, M. 60
Verbik, L. 45, 51
Vietnam 17
Virginia Commonwealth University 49
visas 22

Wang, L. 76
Wang, M. L. 82
Wang, S. 39
Weick, K. E. 70
Weill Cornell Medical College 49
Welch, A. R. 81, 84
whole-person education model 68–9, 70
Wildavsky, B. 60, 63
withdrawal and penalization mechanisms 12–13, 35
World Trade Organization (WTO) 20, 47, 48, 80, 82
Wu, W. G. 64
Wuhan University 48

Xia, B. B. 82
Xiamen University 24, 36, 40
Xi'an Jiaotong Liverpool University 63, 96, 99–113
Xi'an University 66
Xiao, G. X. 81
Xu, X. 47, 48

Yang Fujia 48, 103, 106
Yang, P. P. 37
Yang, R. 80, 81

Zaheer, S. 97
Zee, S. Y. 70
Zha, Q. 82
Zhang, L. 63, 80
Zhang, M. X. 63, 80
Zhejiang University 65, 66
Zhong, B. L. 82
Zhu, Y. X. 34
Zimmerman, M. A. 97, 100